A gift has been made by:

Jerry Baldwin

In honor of

Sherry Baldwin

DOG IS MY
COPILOT

DOG IS MY COPILOT

**Rescue Tales of Flying Dogs,
Second Chances, and the Hero
Who Might Live Next Door**

PATRICK REGAN

**Andrews McMeel
Publishing, LLC**
Kansas City • Sydney • London

Andrews McMeel Publishing, LLC
an Andrews McMeel Universal company
1130 Walnut Street, Kansas City, Missouri 64106

www.andrewsmcmeel.com

12 13 14 15 16 SHO 10 9 8 7 6 5 4 3 2 1

ISBN: 978-1-4494-0760-5

Library of Congress Control Number: 2011932645

ATTENTION: SCHOOLS AND BUSINESSES
Andrews McMeel books are available at quantity discounts with bulk purchase for educational, business, or sales promotional use. For information, please e-mail the Andrews McMeel Publishing Special Sales Department: specialsales@amuniversal.com

Cover photo: "Chipper" awaits takeoff in Evanston, Wyoming. He was en route to a Border Collie rescue in Glenrock, Wyoming. Photo by Jill Clover.

Page ii: "Penny," a rescued Pitbull with Courtnee Mulroy in Onawa, Iowa: Photo by Wendee Mulroy.

FOR ANYONE WHO HAS EVER
HELPED GIVE A DOG A BETTER LIFE

"O TO SPEED WHERE THERE
IS SPACE ENOUGH AND
AIR ENOUGH AT LAST!"

—Walt Whitman

CONTENTS

ACKNOWLEDGMENTS

For every dog there's a story; and for every story in this book there are multiple people who helped me tell it. Though the names are too numerous to list here, I owe a huge debt of gratitude to every pilot, rescuer, transport coordinator, and adopter who shared his or her favorite rescue tale with me.

Certain people must be recognized by name. This book began, as Pilots N Paws did, with Debi Boies and Jon Wehrenberg. Your generosity, spirit, and commitment to a worthy cause will forever be an inspiration. Thank you for trusting me to share the story.

Among the many pilots and rescue volunteers interviewed for this book, several warrant special mention: Lynnette Bennett, Mary Vitt, Stephanie Murphy, Amy Heinz, Mala Brady, Alla McGeary, and Teka Clark—if reincarnation exists, I'd like to come back as one of your dogs. Pilots Jeff Bennett, Jim Bordoni, Jim Carney, Brett Grooms, Rhonda Miles, Robin Lee, Sarah Owens, Pete Howell, Mike Gerdes, and Sam Taylor provided invaluable high-altitude perspective. Safe skies to you always.

The photos in this book appear through the generosity of dozens of different photographers. Thanks to all of you, and special thanks to Jim Carney and Linda Gail Stevens for providing particularly powerful shots.

Thanks to the editorial and creative team at Andrews McMeel Publishing, especially Patty Rice and Holly Ogden, for sticking with me through a logistically challenging book. Thanks also to my twin fonts of publishing wisdom: Michael Reagan and Tom Thornton.

Finally, love and thanks to Patty Regan, my first reader since first grade, and to Sarah, Will, and Luke, who perform the nifty trick of keeping me grounded while encouraging me to fly.

—Patrick Regan, 2011

DOG IS MY
COPILOT

PART ONE

A DREAM OF FLIGHT

The altimeter's hands spin slowly, steadily clockwise. When the dial indicates 3,500 feet, the pilot levels off, adjusts the plane's throttle and fuel mixture, and trims her for cruise flight. His gaze alternately shifts from the instrument panel to the cloudless blue sky beyond the windscreen. The earth below is a patchwork of geometric forms—farm fields rendered in browns, grays, and irrigated greens. Stock ponds, broad-roofed barns, clumps of trees, and straight ribbons of roads—some paved, some not—are all easy to pick out at this altitude.

The pilot breaks the silence, and with it the low-level intensity that accompanies even routine takeoff. "It's OK, girl," he says, "You're all right now." With eyes still fixed on the horizon, he reaches his right hand back between the small plane's two front seats and finds the shoulder of his backseat passenger. She turns forward, pushing a furry muzzle into the pilot's hand. She'd been looking out the window too, wondering, perhaps, exactly how she ended up here.

To answer the question, you have to go back a ways. It all began with Carly—a gentle, intelligent Doberman pinscher, and an "old soul" from the day she was born. That's how Debi Boies remembers her. Debi and her husband, Bob, had raised Carly from a pup. With acres to run and the company of two other dogs and a stable of Morgan horses, her life on the Boieses' South Carolina farm should have been a charmed one. But when she was still young, Carly was accidentally poisoned when she drank rainwater from a not-quite-empty pesticide bucket left out at the peach farm next door. Within hours, the big, boisterous black-and-tan was foaming at the mouth and, as Boies painfully recalls, "losing fluid from every opening in her body." Though rushed to the vet and given fluid intravenously, she was slipping fast and not expected to survive the night.

"I stayed up all night with her," remembers Boies. "She was wrapped in blankets and on a heating pad with warm IVs going into her, but she was still cold to the touch." The dog never stopped looking at Boies. "I kept telling her, 'You can do this, girl. You can make it through.'"

During the overnight vigil, Boies's mind played through the three short years of Carly's life. And sometimes it wandered further, to other animals she had known and loved over her own lifetime—horses, cats, rabbits, chickens, and many, many dogs. But Carly was different. "She was a once-in-a-lifetime animal," says Boies. "She was my heartdog."

Carly survived that critical night and went on to live a good, long life for a Doberman. She battled dilated cardiomyopathy in her later years, and then in 2007, at age twelve, succumbed to large-cell leukemia—a long-term effect, Boies suspects, of the pesticide poisoning that occurred back when she was three.

Debi Boies is a nurse by profession and an animal lover by nature. She grew up in a suburb of Akron, Ohio, and her passion was obvious from an early age. When Debi was a toddler, her mother always worried when dogs were around. "She was terrified that I was going to get bit in the face," explains Boies, "because I would just go right up to any animal I saw. I was born loving animals." Despite her mother's fears, Boies's parents nurtured her love of animals, and gave her a childhood filled with loving and well-loved pets.

As an adult, Boies developed a special fondness for Dobermans, and over the years has spent countless hours working for Doberman rescue groups. She was an original board member of the national nonprofit Doberman Assistance Network (DAN) and served as that organization's intake coordinator for its first two years.

"I feel strongly that it is our responsibility, as humans, to be the guardians for animals others have abandoned, abused, or simply can no longer care for. If we don't, then who will?"

—*Debi Boies, Pilots N Paws cofounder*

A few months after losing Carly, Boies reached out to her network of Doberman rescue friends. She put the word out that she was looking for a new dog. A short time later she heard from a friend at a Doberman rescue in Tallahassee, Florida. She told Boies about a dog that desperately needed a home.

"This dog had been pulled from a high-kill shelter about three months earlier," remembers Boies. "He had every parasite imaginable. He was heartworm-positive. His coat and skin showed multiple signs of abuse, and he had a long abscess scar on his back. He was in very bad condition."

The four-year-old male bore telltale signs of a violent life. The rescue volunteer told Boies that his teeth had been filed down until they were completely flat on top. "He had almost certainly been used as a 'bait dog,'" says Boies. A bait dog is used to train fighting dogs. They're strong but lack the killer instinct of more aggressive fighters, so they're used as sparring partners—or more accurately, live practice dummies for dogs bred and trained to kill. A bait dog's teeth are filed down to limit the damage it can do to the "more valuable" fighters. This young brown-and-black Doberman also had white hairs sprouting at multiple spots on its head—another indication of past physical trauma. "White hairs will grow back in on a dark-haired animal after a serious skin injury," explains Boies.

The more she heard, the more certain she became that this dog should be Carly's successor. But he was five hundred miles away in Tallahassee. Debi and Bob belong to a motor coach owners group, and she put out an e-mail alert to its members to see if anyone happened to be driving north and would be willing to ferry a four-legged passenger. Initially, she got no takers. But a few days later, she received an e-mail that caught her completely off guard.

"I got a message from Jon Wehrenberg, a friend in Tennessee who happens to be a private pilot, and it said, 'How about if I fly down and pick him up for you?'" recalls Boies. "I read it . . . and then I *reread* it, and thought, '*What?*'"

Boies asked Wehrenberg if he was serious. "I'll never forget what he said: 'Pilots love to fly. We're always looking for a reason. How about if I come pick up your husband in Greenville, and we'll go down to Florida and pick up the pup. I'd be happy to do it.'" Still incredulous at her friend's generosity, Boies replied, "Sure! Go for it."

A few days later, Wehrenberg arrived back in Greenville, greeting his friend with the rescued Doberman, and with a question. "He asked, 'Is there a big need to move rescue animals?'" Having been involved in the transport of dogs for years through her work with various rescue groups, Boies replied, "Jon, you have no idea."

Wehrenberg wasn't alone in his ignorance of the nationwide, grassroots network of animal shelter workers and rescue volunteers that has for many years been quietly coordinating the transportation of otherwise doomed animals to places—hundreds,

Pilots N Paws cofounders Jon Wehrenberg and Debi Boies.

sometimes thousands of miles away—where they are more likely to find a permanent home. Animal transports of this sort have gone on for decades, but the Internet
has been a game changer. Online forums, chat groups, and social media have provided the perfect way for rescues, shelters, and potential adopters to find one another.
The technology has effectively "nationalized" animal rescue, making it possible for an
unwanted "death row" dog in a Statesboro, Georgia, animal shelter to find a loving
home in Skowhegan, Maine.

But communication has been the easy part. The physical movement of animals
via a network of volunteer drivers has always been the real challenge.

"Up until this point, we had moved these animals by car, and that's generally one
driver per hour and a car change every hour for the animals," explains Boies. "It's very
stressful for the animals and one break in the human chain—one late rendezvous—can
wreck the whole thing." Having herself once coordinated a 1,500-mile ground transport
with sixteen different drivers and an overnight stay, Boies was intimately familiar with
the complicated logistics and inherent problems with over-the-road animal transport.

Jon Wehrenberg listened intently as Boies outlined the arduous business of volunteer animal transport. But he became even more engaged—shocked even—when she
started reeling off statistics regarding animal shelters and euthanasia. Of the approximately eight million animals that enter shelters each year, more than half are ultimately euthanized. In the southern United States, where both Jon and Debi live, the

euthanasia rate in shelters hovers near 70 percent. Only 10 percent of the animals received by shelters have been spayed or neutered.

Before parting ways, Boies directed Wehrenberg to a few ground transportation Web sites where he could learn more. Back on the ground in Tennessee a few hours later, Wehrenberg began a crash-course education in animal rescue and transport.

"I became a lurker," says Wehrenberg. "It was an absolute revelation to me to look at these sites and discover what was going on. We have two shelter animals, but I didn't even know there were things like animal rescues. I didn't know there were people who work very hard to pull animals from shelters and get them moved to other locations."

For several weeks, Wehrenberg monitored the animal transport forums. He watched the boards with a pilot's eye, noting distances and noticing patterns. He observed that specific routes were more common than others. Most obvious to him was the disproportionate number of requests to move animals from the South and Southeast to the Northeast or Midwest.

He was awed by the obvious dedication of the rescue coordinators who planned routes, coordinated drivers, and scheduled transfers, but he could not get past the fact that there had to be a better way.

A retired entrepreneur and a general-aviation pilot for more than thirty years, Wehrenberg had long used a small airplane for business. "I used a plane to commute, so to me a plane is nothing more than transportation," he explains. "It's not a recreation vehicle—it's a business tool. I think of it as a pickup truck or a car." But Wehrenberg

also knew that an airplane was something more—a way to compress time. The advantages of using light aircraft to move rescue animals grew more obvious in his mind as he watched the never-ending parade of online posts requesting transports.

"I'm sitting here looking at these requests for transport from a pilot and plane owner's perspective. When Debi told me how many millions of animals were being euthanized, I said, 'Oh, no. Not if I can help it.'"

—*Jon Wehrenberg, Pilots N Paws cofounder*

"There wasn't a eureka moment," says Wehrenberg, "It was more of a *holy shit!* moment. To move Debi's dog it would have taken eight drivers all day and the puppy would have been handled at rest areas along the interstate and potentially have the risk of getting loose and running away."

Boies remembers a phone call from Wehrenberg a few weeks after he delivered her rescue Doberman. "He called and said, 'You know, Debi, we really have to do something about this. If we can connect these transport needs with general-aviation pilots, I really think we could make a difference.'"

Neither Debi Boies nor Jon Wehrenberg knew at that moment what their animal-rescue endeavor would look like, how it would be formed, or how it would function. But Boies did have an idea about what to name it. "I said, 'How about if we call it Pilots N Paws?'" she remembers. "Jon said, 'Sounds good to me.' So off we went."

It would take many more weeks of work to get the program off the ground, but at that moment, Pilots N Paws was cleared for takeoff. In the cramped kennels of animal shelters all across the country, tails began to wag.

PART TWO

LIFTOFF . . . AND NAVIGATION

The story of Pilots N Paws is ultimately the story of two worlds coming together. PNP's founders each came into this union representing one of these two worlds. Debi Boies was a longtime animal rescuer and advocate. Jon Wehrenberg was a private pilot with more than thirty years of experience in the cockpit. Boies and Wehrenberg met each other through a common interest not connected to either animals or airplanes. But their meeting—and subsequent creation of Pilots N Paws—has led to a continued "overlapping" of two different worlds. This convergence has, in the years from 2008 to 2012, resulted in thousands of animals being spared euthanasia.

Before that could happen, Wehrenberg and Boies—the pilot and the rescuer—had to educate each other about their own esoteric worlds.

"She was not aware of general aviation or the extent to which pilots would jump into this type of thing," says Wehrenberg. "She had to take my word on that at face value, and I had to take what she told me about rescues at face value because I didn't have a clue about that side of it. So the two of us were going back and forth translating things to each other. I learned about rescues and the difficulty they have with transports, and she started hearing from me things from the pilot's perspective—things we would be concerned about such as weight and balance, weather, things of that nature."

"General aviation" is a term unfamiliar to most nonpilots. What it means, most simply, is the world of aviation that exists outside of commercial airlines, military, and scheduled cargo flights. General-aviation airports and airfields are typically quite small but serve a broad range of customers, including private and sport fliers, flight trainers, air ambulances and police aircraft, and small-business and charter jets. There are more than five thousand "GA" airports across the United States, the majority of them unmanned.

> **"There's no pilot I've ever been aware of who feels he has enough opportunity to fly, so we put two and two together and said, 'Hey, if we can merge the rescues who are looking for transports with pilots who are looking for an opportunity to fly, we might have something here.'"**
>
> —*Jon Wehrenberg*

From the beginning, PNP's founders were determined to keep things simple. "I have to laugh when people refer to PNP as an 'organization,'" says Wehrenberg. "We

Top: PNP pilot Brett Grooms (r) with Mallory Corder and a canine passenger. Bottom: Volunteer in-flight animal wrangler Gina Austin does backseat duty for PNP pilot Jim Carney.

PNP pilot Mark Kozak with rambunctious cargo.

set this up as a bulletin board—nothing else—a place where the two could come together, and we did that for a very specific reason. We knew that, as this thing grew, there would be a tremendous need for coordination unless we just let people arm wrestle among themselves to work out the transports."

Since the beginning, that's essentially how PNP has worked. Animal rescuers post the details of their transport requests on the PNP Ride Board (what Wehrenberg refers to as the "bulletin board"), including vital information such as departure and arrival cities, size of dog, special needs, etc.

Pilots who've signed up as PNP volunteers are asked to check the board regularly to see if there's a flight—or one leg of a multileg transport—that they are able and willing to take on. If a pilot sees a "doable" flight, he or she contacts the rescue poster directly and details are worked out between both parties. There is no central command. No set schedule. No minimum commitment for pilots. And no distance limit—although the average for any single flight is usually around 300 nautical miles (roughly 350 ground miles).

One other thing: There are no fees. Pilots donate their time, their aircraft, and their fuel expenses for every mission they take on. Because Pilots N Paws has been set up as a registered 501(c)(3) charity, this is nonnegotiable. "We can't accept money. We can't accept any kind of gratuity. We can't even accept lunch from a rescue," says

Wehrenberg. Pilots can, if they choose to, file their expenses as a charitable donation. "That's frosting on the cake," says Wehrenberg. "It's not why the pilot is doing it, but if he's going to be doing it, at least he gets a little benefit out of it."

In a very real way, Wehrenberg was the "test pilot" for PNP. One of his first challenges in that capacity was convincing a skeptical rescue community that his offer to fly rescue dogs was genuine and free of hidden motives. Subsequent to flying Debi Boies's Doberman, he had flown several other transports for the Doberman Assistance Network—all of them set up by Boies, and all of them successful. But he found that when he tried to "fly solo" and set up a transport without Boies's express endorsement, he met with resistance.

"I responded to a posting on Yahoo! for a [ground] transport from Chattanooga to Jamestown, New York," he says. "It was a two-day transport with at least a dozen legs. I went on the forum and said, 'Hey, I'll do the whole thing in my plane.'" The response was underwhelming. "Dead silence," he recalls. "So I communicated directly with the coordinator, and assured her that I would do in 2¾ hours what was going to take two days. Still no embracing of the concept. They just couldn't accept that I didn't have an ulterior motive."

"The concept" was no doubt radical to the person setting up the transport. Maybe it all seemed too easy. "Maybe," jokes Boies, "they thought we were puppy thieves."

Wehrenberg persisted. "I never had to work so hard to get folks to agree to let me do a transport," he says. "I finally convinced her by telling her that I did, in fact, have an ulterior motive. I grew up in Jamestown, New York, and my daughter lives there. I told the coordinator that I wanted to do the transport not only because it would save the pups (there were four), but because I could have lunch with Wendi. Apparently that convinced her that I wasn't going to steal the dogs."

The transport came off without a hitch. "It gave me credibility, because I now had references," says Wehrenberg, "and it proved to my satisfaction that we as pilots could easily do what rescuers were trying, not always successfully, to do with cars. We had to gain the trust of rescues, and that first flight without Debi's involvement was the breakthrough. It was like knocking over the first domino. After that one came off, I knew that PNP was a go."

"I've flown as many as seventeen animals at one time in my plane. It stinks like a barn after doing that . . . but I don't care, because that's seventeen animals that ain't gonna get euthanized."

—Jon Wehrenberg

Having won the trust of animal-rescue coordinators and built a rudimentary online forum for pilots and rescues, Boies and Wehrenberg moved on to their next challenge—attracting pilots. "Neither Jon nor I ever worried that we'd have a shortage of transport requests," says Boies, "but we did spend a lot of time talking about how to spread the word to pilots."

The two turned to the old-fashioned local media to get their story out. Wehrenberg had a friend who worked as a columnist for his hometown newspaper in Knoxville. He told him about PNP and the journalist (also an animal lover) was interested. But Wehrenberg wanted to make sure that they didn't end up with a piddling public-interest story buried somewhere on page twelve. "He worked with me and told me how to get the editor of the paper to do a story of substantial prominence," says Wehrenberg. "We worked on it for about three months and ultimately succeeded in getting the *Knoxville News Sentinel* to do an extremely large Sunday feature story on PNP. They sent a reporter on a transport with a pilot. They spoke to animal-rescue volunteers. They shot a video to accompany the story. And that laid the foundation for all the media coverage that would follow."

USA Today picked up on the story, also shooting a video segment to go along with a full page of print coverage. That opened the national-media floodgates. In ensuing months, in addition to countless stories on local network affiliates and in local newspapers large and small, *NBC Nightly News with Brian Williams*, *World News Tonight with Charles Gibson*, *Fox News*, *CBS Evening News with Katie Couric*, and ABC's *Good Morning America*

Top: PNP cofounder Jon Weherenberg and passenger.
Bottom: PNP cofounder Debi Boies.

all filmed and aired PNP stories. The story of death-row dogs bound for better homes via small aircraft proved to be irresistible to the press.

To augment this surprising media juggernaut, Boies and Wehrenberg also reached out to pilots "where they live," manning a booth at air shows, posting notices in GA publications, and leaving promotional fliers in GA airports.

Word-of-mouth referrals were probably the best promotional tool of all. Pilots talk to pilots—in online forums, through aero club events, and just hanging around at America's thousands of small airfields. Pilots N Paws began as a curiosity, and fairly quickly became a not-so-unusual topic of pilot conversation.

Kansas-based pilot Sarah Owens learned about PNP from an article in an aviation magazine. "I had obtained my private pilot's license a year and a half earlier, and wanted to do something more than fly for the 'hundred dollar hamburger,'" she says, employing a term common among pilots. When pilots want to take a short flight—to log hours, to practice, or just for fun—they will sometimes fly in to a small airport, fifty to one hundred miles away, have lunch, and fly home. The fuel cost for such pleasure flights (these days well over $100) inspired the colorful idiom. Pete Howell, a PNP volunteer based in St. Paul, Minnesota, uses a different colloquialism to describe flying for flying's sake. "'Boring holes in the sky,' is what some people call it," says Howell. "It's much nicer to have a mission."

PNP pilot Sarah Owens loads up eight Lab puppies in Lawrence, Kansas. Rescue volunteer Rhonda Schademann helps ride herd.

As Owens, Howell, and hundreds of others signed up for PNP transports, it became clear that Jon Wehrenberg's instincts about pilots' willingness to get involved were dead on.

"I've noticed that airplane guys are typically dog guys, too."

— *Pete Howell, PNP pilot*

By the end of 2011—after nearly four years and countless hours of hard work by Boies and Wehrenberg—more than two thousand pilots were registered with Pilots N Paws.

Mission accomplished? Not by a long shot, according to the founders. "Our goal is to get ten thousand pilots," says Boies. "We want enough pilots so that no request goes unanswered. There are between three hundred and four hundred thousand general-aviation pilots in this country, so if we can get just 3 or 4 percent, we're there."

As in any organization, levels of involvement vary. For some pilots, financial constraints and busy schedules allow only occasional rescue flights. Others have enthusiastically become the "heavy lifters" of airborne animal transport. (Wehrenberg is among them. He celebrated transporting his five hundredth dog in the summer of 2010.) Most pilots fall somewhere in between—flying a rescue mission every few weeks or once a month. But no matter how often they fly, PNP pilots are universally enthusiastic about the rewards.

Left: PNP pilot Ron Lee preps for takeoff. Right: A sign in the window of PNP pilot Rhonda Mills's plane.

Jeff Bennett is a semiretired businessman based in the Florida Keys. At this point, he isn't sure exactly how many PNP missions he's flown, but in the spring of 2011, he transported his five hundredth "critter." "I've learned that there are two types of transports," Bennett says. "You have transports where you're taking a dog out of a kill shelter and flying him to a rescue. In those cases, it's a personal thing, because you're not dealing with anybody except the shelters and rescues, and you know for a fact that

PNP pilot Patrick Lofvenholm with passenger Rommel.

you're saving these dogs' lives. The other kind is where you fly a dog to an adoptive home and you get to see the joy on people's faces when they receive their new family member, so each one has its own reward." He then adds, "I gotta admit, even though it's great seeing people with their new family member, I think moving them out of kill shelters is probably more rewarding to me."

> **"These dogs know—I mean they absolutely know—that they're being rescued. Don't ask me how. Every rescue I've spoken to about this has agreed with me that somehow the animals know that when they're pulled from a shelter, and put on a plane and delivered to another rescue, their whole attitude changes, as though they know they don't have to be scared anymore. They're going to be safe. I can't explain it, but it's like they sense that everything is going to be okay."**
>
> —*Jon Wehrenberg*

There are less obvious rewards, too. For some pilots, the best part of PNP is meeting and working with their collaborators in the animal-rescue community.

"Pilots definitely build personal relationships with our ground counterparts, and that to me is one of the most interesting things that PNP has been able to accomplish," says South Carolina–based pilot Brett Grooms. "It has brought thousands of people from varying backgrounds together to help our furry friends, but along the way it's also unknowingly created lifelong friendships among a diverse group of people who might otherwise never have met."

For thousands of volunteers on the rescue side, working with PNP has given them insight into a subculture that they would likely never have otherwise seen. "There's a stereotype of people with planes," says Boies. "For a lot of us it's a somewhat mysterious culture. People assume they're all wealthy. That's actually far from the truth. They are people united by a common love of aviation. For people who feel that desire deeply enough, they'll find a way to fly."

Robin Lee perfectly fits that description. Lee is a general-aviation pilot in Seattle. She doesn't own her own plane, but when she signs on for a PNP mission, she rents one for a day. Lee works three different jobs (all in the aviation field), partially to fund her

love of flying. "My passions are aviation and animals," she says. "[Renting a plane] to help dogs in need is worth every penny to me."

Mike Gannon is a PNP pilot based in the sparsely populated northwestern corner of Kansas. A former air traffic controller, Gannon bought a 1969 Cessna a few years ago when his brother, living back on the family farm in Vermont, was diagnosed with terminal cancer. He uses the plane to make trips back east to visit. "It's three hard days by pickup truck or nine hours in that Cessna," says Gannon in a deep, gruff voice. "So that's generally what I use it for." He never makes the trip without first checking the PNP transport board to see if a rescue dog needs a ride east. He also frequently shuttles dogs through what he calls "a dead zone" for rescue flights between central Kansas and Colorado's Front Range. All kinds of people fly planes for all kinds of reasons. Pilots N Paws provides them with a very compelling one.

When the airplane was invented, it shrunk the world. Airplanes still do that. When PNP was founded, it brought two worlds together. Preconceived notions are laid to rest as pilots and rescuers come together, unified in their mission to save animals. Since early 2008, that germ of an idea—to bring private pilots and animal rescuers together—has grown into an "organization" like no other.

Small aircraft have been around for more than a hundred years now, but it's still the rare person who doesn't take notice when a small propeller plane passes overhead. Hearing the faint thrum of an engine, we instinctively turn our eyes skyward to search out that tiny white cross moving slowly across the ocean of blue. We are transported for just a moment, caught up in the mystery. *Who's up there? Where are they going?*

We on the ground never know for sure. But the next time you look up to see a small plane tracking across the sky, keep in mind that there may well be a pair of curious and hope-filled eyes looking out that plane's window—eyes that don't belong to the person flying the plane. A passenger of an entirely different sort may be gazing out and seeing for the first time the broad expanse of Earth unfolding below, and imagining a new life far from the one left behind.

Behind every flight, there's a story. . . .

PART THREE

FLIGHT TALES

CASSIDY
RIDES AGAIN

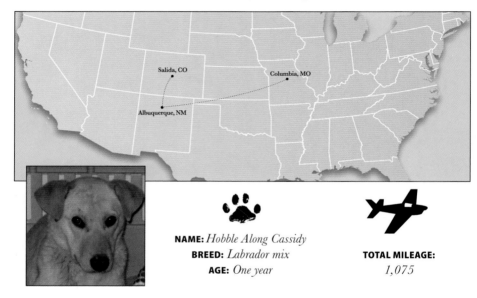

NAME: *Hobble Along Cassidy*
BREED: *Labrador mix*
AGE: *One year*

TOTAL MILEAGE:
1,075

ROUTE:

Salida, Colorado–Albuquerque, New Mexico
Albuquerque, New Mexico–Columbia, Missouri

I n the Navajo Nation, stray and abandoned dogs are so common as to be part of the landscape. As an educational audiologist for the Bureau of Indian Education, Mary Vitt regularly visits schools all across the vast Eastern Navajo Reservation. She sees "rez dogs" everywhere she goes. "They're usually skin and bones," she says.

At her home in Crownpoint, New Mexico, Vitt keeps a binder full of pictures of the dogs—and a few cats—she's picked up, fostered, and helped place in homes over her ten years on the job. She worries over the ones she hasn't been able to help. Near one of her schools there's an abandoned graffiti-covered building with a large hole in

Mary Vitt has rescued dozens of strays on the Navajo reservation in New Mexico. She found Hobble Along Cassidy scared, skittish, and injured in 2010.

one wall. A group of strays moves in and out, using the building for shelter. Vitt and a colleague regularly leave piles of dry food for the pack, which she affectionately calls the Hole-in-the-Wall Gang.

In the spring of 2010, Vitt spotted a new member among the motley assortment of dogs—a young yellow Lab mix. Obviously injured, the small dog "kind of scooted to get around," says Vitt. Scared and skittish, she kept a wary distance from the pack and from Vitt, but with help from a friend the veteran rescuer was able to scoop up the injured dog in a blanket. She took her home and cared for her the best she could while she looked for help. She named the gimpy dog Hobble Along Cassidy.

A local vet examined the pup and offered amputation as the only option for its badly damaged front leg. But Vitt wasn't ready to accept such a drastic solution. She knew it would make finding a permanent home for Cassidy all the more difficult. Through online networking, Vitt found a veterinarian in Missouri who was willing to perform the complicated surgery needed to save the dog's leg at a greatly reduced cost.

Top: Cassidy rests after her initial vet exam in New Mexico. Above: Colorado-based pilots Greg and Sharon Gempler flew Cassidy all the way from Albuquerque, New Mexico, to Columbia, Missouri.

A New Mexico–based rescue, Luvin' Labs, helped Vitt with fundraising for the surgery, but a commercial flight to Missouri was too expensive for Vitt or the rescue to cover.

Vitt discovered Pilots N Paws while doing an Internet search for animal transport. She'd never heard of the group before but wrote up a post requesting transport to Missouri and crossed her fingers. "I really didn't expect a response," she remembers.

A few days later, hope for Hobble Along Cassidy arrived in the form of a phone call from Sharon Gempler, who, along with her husband, Greg, volunteered to fly from their home in central Colorado to pick up the injured dog and fly her all the way from Albuquerque to Columbia, Missouri—a total distance of more than 1,800 air miles. Vitt was dumbfounded. Of the Gemplers she simply says, "They are awesome people."

After several reschedules and a near scrub because of inclement weather, the trip came off a few days later. On the ground in Columbia, Dr. James ("Jimi") Cook and his staff at the University of Missouri Veterinary Medical Teaching Hospital took over. Examining the patient, they discovered all her toes on one foot were broken and a different leg was fractured.

The surgery was long and compli-cated, but a few days later, Mary Vitt received an e-mail from Dr. Cook:

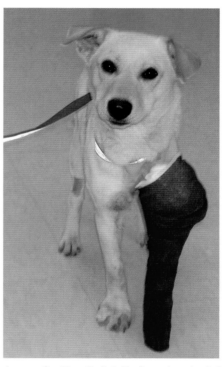

Cassidy is doing great—have to drop the "Hobble-Along" part of her name now!! She is all healed up, spayed, and allowed to return to full function!! She has a GREAT home and is a NEAT dog!!

The doctor attached a short video clip—just a few seconds of a pretty yel-low Lab walking down a clinic corridor, a bright purple cast encasing her front left leg. The great home he mentioned was with one of his veterinary students who had decided to adopt Cassidy fol-lowing the surgery.

Back on the Eastern Navajo Reser-vation, Mary Vitt still worries over the Hole-in-the-Wall Gang. She has names for all the regulars. Radar, Stella, Motley,

A post-op Cassidy walks the halls of a veterinary hospital in Columbia, Missouri.

and Pretty Boy Floyd are all still out there—part of the endless string of unwanteds that scrounge and struggle to survive in a harsh environment. Not long after Vitt res-cued Cassidy, a small dog from the gang was hit by a car and killed. Vitt hadn't decided on a name for him yet.

"There are times I get very angry and depressed," she concedes. "It's so hard to see the need and not have resources to help them all. I remind myself that I can't save the world, but rescue means the world to the one dog you can help."

HOME AT LAST, HOME FOR GOOD

NAME: *Sammie*
BREED: *Golden retriever*
AGE: *Three years*

TOTAL MILEAGE:
733

ROUTE:
Knoxville, Tennessee–Orange, Virginia
Orange, Virginia–Hartford, Connecticut

Turned out of one home in rural eastern Tennessee and neglected by a second, Sammie spent much of her time wandering along a nearby highway. By the time she was spotted by an animal-rescue volunteer, in December 2009, she had been hobbled by a broken bone in her right leg and lost sight in one eye, almost certainly the result of being hit by a car.

With permission from her indifferent owners, the rescuer took the three-year-old golden retriever to Heartland Golden Retriever Rescue in Knoxville, Tennessee. After three months of care and therapy—including regular hydrotherapy sessions where

Sammie exercised her badly atrophied leg in a swimming pool—she had recovered enough to be offered for adoption.

Pauline Stevens, who runs Heartland, remembers Sammie as "a true golden in every sense—her temperament, looks, size—and her affectionate nature. . . . She would literally lean into you for more love," recalls Stevens. But the veteran rescue volunteer also got a sense of Sammie's mettle. "She wanted so badly to please, and even though it must have hurt her to do some of the things we asked her to do [for physical therapy], she was still willing to give it her all." Under the care of Heartland; the Lenoir City Animal Clinic, where Sammie was boarded; and Barkside Lodge, where she underwent her hydrotherapy, Sammie, according to Stevens, "blossomed into a beautiful dog."

Top: Sammie undergoes hydrotherapy in Tennessee. Bottom: Transferring Sammie in Virginia. Pictured: PNP pilots Tom Nalle (kneeling) and Martin Hobson (right). Nalle's daughter and Hobson's son assisted on the flights.

Not long after, at home in Massachusetts, Kristen Smolski saw Sammie on Heartland's Web site. Touched by her story and her smile, Smolski submitted an adoption application. "People joke that it's easier to adopt a baby than one of our dogs," says Stevens of her rescue's stringent application requirements. But in Smolski, she sensed a perfect match for Sammie.

Pilot Tom Nalle is a friend and neighbor of Pauline Stevens in Knoxville, and has helped her transport many dogs to the New England area. In early March 2010, Nalle and his daughter, Caitlin, loaded Sammie into his Mooney M20E in Knoxville, and flew to Orange, Virginia, where he met up with another PNP volunteer, Martin Hobson. Hobson and his son flew Sammie to Hartford, Connecticut.

> "The evening before the flight, I knelt down next to her to give her a hug. She moved up close and leaned heavily against me, placed her head on my shoulder, and just sat there completely still with her weight against me. I'll never forget that. She was so happy just to be held. Knowing her history gave me a sense that she was truly a remarkable animal."
>
> —*Tom Nalle, PNP pilot*

Top: A run-in wtih a car left Sammie blind in one eye.
Bottom: Sammie and Caitlin Nalle enjoy a moment in the sun.

On the ramp in Hartford, Kristen Smolski met Sammie for the first time. "I don't think I slept at all the night before," recalls Smolski. "I was like a kid at Christmas." Once home, Sammie met her new big sister, a five-year-old golden named Harley. Within minutes they were inseparable—two big, boisterous girls lost in a game of tug-of-war in the backyard.

To Pauline Stevens, Tom Nalle, Martin Hobson, and Pilots N Paws, Kristen Smolski will be forever grateful. "I don't have any kids, so my dogs are my children, and basically they brought together a family. That's how I look at it."

Top: Tom Nalle and daughter Caitlin shuttle Sammie to Virginia. Bottom: Sammie meets new mom Kristen Smolski as rescue volunteer Susan Simon and Abby Simon-Plumb look on.

APPETITE FOR AVIATION

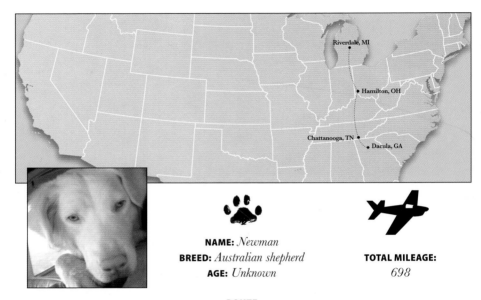

NAME: *Newman*
BREED: *Australian shepherd*
AGE: *Unknown*

TOTAL MILEAGE:
698

ROUTE:
*Dacula, Georgia–Chattanooga, Tennessee**
Chattanooga, Tennessee–Hamilton, Ohio
Hamilton, Ohio–Riverdale, Michigan

Tennessee-based pilot Rhonda Miles has flown more than fifty dogs on behalf of Pilots N Paws, but one particular passenger stands out. Newman was a deaf Australian shepherd on a multileg trip north to Michigan. Miles tells the story of their brief but memorable time together:

* Ground (car) transport leg

Newman was my only passenger, so I let him roam around the back of the plane. He was a sweet boy, and would put his head on my shoulder and ride looking out the front. Every now and then he would wander to the back and lie down for a bit, but he always returned. When I checked in with Cincinnati Center, they vectored me around the east side of their airspace and then toward Hamilton. They told me to let them know when I had Hamilton's airport in sight. I reached over to my right seat to pick up the printout of the airport diagram and the airport frequencies, but couldn't find it. I looked in the back and Newman was eating it! I had to call Cincinnati and say, "This is going to sound stupid, but this is a dog-rescue flight, and my dog ate my paperwork. Can you give me frequencies?" . . . Over the radio, I could hear the controllers laughing as they helped me out.

Miles reports that Newman went on to an alpaca farm, where he started learning sign language. "I always wondered what the sign is for 'Cough it up, Bud.'"

Rhonda Miles and Newman.

ANGEL GETS HER WINGS

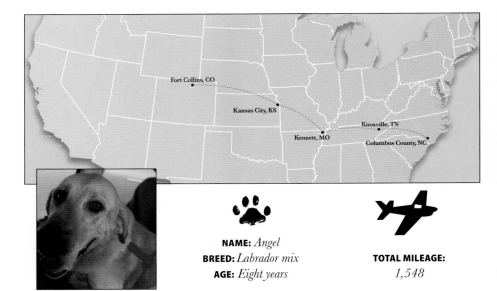

NAME: *Angel*
BREED: *Labrador mix*
AGE: *Eight years*

TOTAL MILEAGE:
1,548

ROUTE:
*Columbus County, North Carolina–Knoxville, Tennessee
Knoxville, Tennessee–Kennett, Missouri
Kennett, Missouri–Kansas City, Kansas
Kansas City, Kansas–Fort Collins, Colorado*

Empathy is the heart of animal rescue—but technology is the central nervous system. The grassroots online network that has grown around the rescue, foster, transport, and adoption of homeless animals would make any political action committee envious. The Internet, Facebook, Yahoo! groups, and pet adoption sites allow millions of committed people to connect across thousands of miles—making it possible for an abandoned dog in North Carolina to find a new home in Colorado within a matter of days. In bottom-line terms, technology allows the gross oversupply of animals in one part of the country to meet keen demand in other parts.

Mala Brady discovered this network by accident in 2009 while signing an online petition protesting an animal cruelty incident in her home state of Colorado.

"When I signed it and read the comments I realized there is a whole network of animal lovers working to save animals," she explains. "There are adopters, rescues, pullers [people who pull the animals from a shelter], transports, crossposters [who post homeless dogs to multiple social-networking sites, forums, and message boards], and ChipIn people [who create and post PayPal ChipIn widgets so others can donate to help cover the various pull fees shelters charge]."

As a devoted animal lover, Brady decided to join the movement. She created a Facebook page dedicated to animal welfare, started "friending" people who seemed the most involved, and soon was crossposting pleas for animals in shelters.

She had become another vital link in the network connecting animals in

Angel takes a preflight peek from Keith Decker's Cessna.

need with willing adopters, but, having a pretty fair-sized rescued menagerie already, she hadn't planned to adopt any animals herself. That changed the day she posted a picture of a dog in the Columbus County, North Carolina, Animal Control shelter.

"It's difficult to describe, but she touched a place deep in my heart," says Brady. "I knew from the minute I saw her she would be our dog."

The dog had no name, only the designation K-38. Brady called the shelter to get more information. The good: The staff said she was very sweet. The bad: She suffered a host of health problems due to owner negligence. Estimated to be around eight years old, she had arthritis in her hips, a severe flea infestation, and poor mobility due to weak hindquarters. She was heartworm-positive. She was also twenty minutes away from her euthanasia deadline.

Brady didn't waste one of those minutes. Reaching out to her rescue network, she arranged to have K-38 pulled. Once pulled, the dog received a cursory vetting with vaccinations and flea treatment. The adoption fee provided for ten days' boarding. Now Brady had to find a way to get the dog halfway across the country to Colorado.

Ground transport would have been physically difficult for a dog of her age and condition, and prohibitively expensive—a commercial flight even more so. Brady had

heard of Pilots N Paws but had never posted to it before. She decided to give it a shot. Two pilots, Jim Carney and Jim Bordoni, each volunteered to fly a leg. Those two took it upon themselves to find two others—Keith Decker and Mitchell Stafford—to complete the transport. Bordoni also arranged a two-night foster in Kansas City, Kansas, before the final leg of the flight. None of the pilots had any previous connection with Mala Brady. Each of them spent hundreds of dollars of their own money to deliver her dog.

Upon landing in Colorado, K-38 got a new name.

"We named her Angel in honor of all of the angels who were a part of her rescue," says Brady. "Everyone involved in her rescue is an angel in my book," she continues, "but the pilots really stand out. They make it possible for animals to be saved by providing the transportation, which is one of the most difficult aspects of rescue. What is most wonderful, though, is that they truly care. I stay in touch with Jim and Jim, and count them as friends."

"If it were not for Jim and Jim's help I would not have been able to do it. They called me, e-mailed me, and told me how to track the flights. They sent pictures of her along the way. I actually felt like I was there, too."

—*Mala Brady*

PNP pilots Jim Carney (left) and Jim Bordoni with Angel.

Angel is thriving in her Colorado home. She's put on weight and muscle. She bounds up the stairs she once struggled to climb and plays with the Brady's four other dogs. In the fall she ferrets out and munches apples fallen from the tree and in winter she gleefully plows her nose through the snow. "It's hard to believe she's the same dog," says Brady.

Brady knows how lucky she and Angel are to have found each other. The effect of her direct experience with PNP was profound. "After posting so many dogs that have suffered at the hands of people who are supposed to be their caregivers, it restores my faith in people," she says. It has also motivated her to "pay it forward." Since adopting Angel, she's helped coordinate several other animal transports through PNP.

"And every one of the pilots," she says, "has been terrific!"

MOJO AND MOM

Marianna, FL

Lakeland, FL

NAME: *Mojo*
BREED: *Dachshund*
AGE: *Four years*

TOTAL MILEAGE:
273

ROUTE:
Marianna, Florida–Lakeland, Florida

For years, Devon and Jill Barger tried in vain to persuade Jill's mother, Mary Palmer, to adopt a dog for companionship. The ninety-five-year-old resisted. "She would always say she wasn't home enough to take care of an animal—which was true until her eyesight went," says Devon.

In recent years, macular degeneration has robbed Mary Palmer of much of her sight. No longer able to drive or live on her own, she moved from Connecticut to Florida to live with her daughter and son-in-law.

As an avid general-aviation pilot, Devon began volunteering to transport animals through Pilots N Paws shortly after the organization was launched in 2008. Flying out of St. Augustine, Florida, with Jill as nonpilot navigator, Devon had transported sixty animals by the end of 2010. Occasionally, his mother-in-law would fly along on their missions.

In January 2010, the Bargers answered a PNP request to transport several dogs from Marianna to Lakeland, Florida. Mary decided to ride along for the scenic flight along Florida's Gulf Coast. Devon remembers the day well—and the perfect opportunity that presented itself.

"It was a full load that day—eight dogs, I think—and we ran out of cages. One little guy that may have been left behind was a buckskin-colored dachshund. He was four years old and had been abandoned at a vet's office by his owners. 'Monroe' arrived in a leather flight jacket with the word 'copilot' embossed on the back. He could not have been cuter or more affectionate. Funny how it turned out, but my mother-in-law's lap was the only empty seat in the house."

Barger continues, taking obvious delight in this story's conclusion. "The two spent the better part of three hours in flight, and they were hooked on each other. Monroe disappeared off the flight manifest and came home with us to St. Augustine."

Monroe, now known as "Mojo" or "Mo," blissfully settled into life in the Barger's mother-in-law suite. He is a constant companion to Mary. They go for afternoon walks when the weather is fine, and spend contented hours in her favorite chair, an antique rocker that, in truth, isn't ideally suited for snuggling. "No matter," says Barger. "Mo perches in her lap, legs dangling, happy as a clam.

"Now the best time of the afternoon is naptime, snuggled up with his new mom," says Barger. "He is well aware of his new mission—to take care of Mom—and he does."

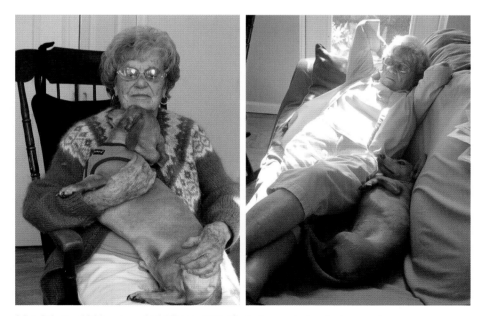

Mary Palmer and Mojo met on a fateful flight in 2010. They've been constant companions ever since.

Though Mo had clearly won Mary's heart, he was long denied his most persistent request—to share her bed at night. Mary held out for months, but eventually, the persuasive dachshund wore her down. As she learned on that fateful flight along the Florida coast, the little guy is hard to resist.

A SWEET
SOUTHERN GIRL

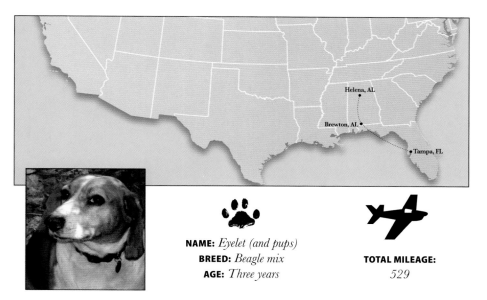

NAME: *Eyelet (and pups)*
BREED: *Beagle mix*
AGE: *Three years*

TOTAL MILEAGE:
529

ROUTE:
*Helena, Alabama–Brewton, Alabama**
Brewton, Alabama–Tampa, Florida

Sixteen-year-old Sawyer Thompson and a friend were out exploring in the woods a few miles from home in Helena, Alabama. As they kicked through the fallen leaves on a November day, the boys' casual conversation came to an abrupt stop. Before them on the ground, on a bed of leaves and litter, lay a small brown dog—a beagle mix—nursing six tiny puppies. They moved in for a closer look, and their initial excitement turned to dismay. "The babies' condition was good," Thompson recalls, "but the mother's was awful. She was skinny and covered with sores."

* Ground (car) transport leg

41

When the dog who would later be called Eyelet was discovered in rural Alabama, she was starving yet continuing to nurse her six puppies.

The dog wasn't a stray, Thompson knew. In fact, he knew who her owner was. He also knew that the animals' lives were in real danger if he didn't do something. He went to the owner's house, "a shack built in the 1800s," and asked if he could take the dogs somewhere safe. "He was kinda iffy at first, but then I told him I would find them good homes," says Thompson, "and he said OK."

For the previous two years, Thompson had volunteered at a local animal rescue, so he knew what to do. He and his friend carefully loaded the frightened animals into his truck and drove them to the home of Sonya Smith.

Smith is the founder and director of Two by Two Rescue, the small volunteer organization in Helena where Thompson had often donated his time. Seeing the emaciated mother dog for the first time, Smith immediately dubbed her "Eyelet," an admittedly unusual name that she goes on to explain.

"I am a southern girl and so is this sweet dog!" says Smith, in a voice fairly dripping Tupelo honey. "My grandmother and mother taught me to sew as a child and one of my favorite cloths was eyelet—a fabric or notion that is very feminine and used a lot in the South. When I first laid eyes on the little beagle momma, she had such a sweet feminine quality to her that I knew she needed a name that communicated that characteristic. Within seconds I thought of Eyelet."

Smith cleaned the puppies up and began tending to Eyelet. She was clearly not well, but the "southern girl" gratefully accepted food and water. Smith's next step was to find help—and a home—for this ragged clan. She posted an urgent SOS to the rescue community. The dogs would all need vetting and, until they could be placed in forever homes, foster care.

Concerned e-mails poured in from across the country, and generous strangers chipped in nearly $500 to cover vet costs. Although malnourished and full of parasites, the little family received a positive prognosis. After just a few days, the three- to four-week-old babies were thriving.

Among the e-mails Smith received in response to her SOS was a particularly welcome one from Kelley Curtis, director of Lucky Ones Rescue, a nonprofit rescue in Tampa, Florida. Curtis agreed to foster the entire family while seeking permanent homes for the pups and their mother.

Through the ever-buzzing network of animal rescuers, Smith learned that a PNP pilot would be flying some dogs out of Alabama that very same week. The pilot, Steve Clegg, had already booked "at least ten other dogs" for passage to Florida that day, but confirmed that he had room for more.

Left: Several months after being rescued by an Alabama teenager, Eyelet poses, fat and happy. Right: One of Eyelet's six pups.

Based in Daytona, Florida, Clegg is a frequent flier for PNP and well-known (and deeply appreciated) by the staffs of several overcrowded and underfunded shelters in Alabama and Georgia. He tries to make a monthly run from those states to Florida rescues willing to take in more dogs, and he's a firm believer in filling his plane. He has carried as many as nineteen dogs at a time in his Piper Aztec.

About a week after Eyelet and her pups were discovered in the Alabama woods, Clegg picked up the forlorn family in Brewton, Alabama. Stephen Kelly, another Two by Two rescue volunteer, had driven them four hours from Helena.

"Eyelet still did not look well—you could see all her ribs," remembers Clegg, "but she was just the sweetest dog. As soon as you looked at her she would start wagging her tail."

Kelley Curtis met Clegg on the ground at Tampa Executive Airport. The puppies had charmed him—"I wanted to take every one of them home with me," he says—but saying good-bye to their mother was even more difficult.

"As I walked Eyelet to her waiting car, I whispered in her ear that she would now get the life she deserved."

With Curtis's help, Eyelet's cute brood all found loving homes easily, but their mother's struggles were not yet over. She was heartworm-positive. Clegg, among others, pitched in for her treatments.

Under Curtis's care, the parasites were eventually purged from Eyelet's system. It had taken more than a year to get the young mother fully well, but by mid-2011, Curtis was nearly ready to make her available for adoption to a forever home—though one sensed it wouldn't be easy for the rescuer to part with this sweet southern girl. "She has a very small growth that needs to be removed," Curtis reports, "and then she will finally be put up for adoption . . . but in the meantime, I think she is quite content here."

PNP pilots rarely see their canine passengers once a transport is finished, but several months after flying Eyelet and her puppies, Steve Clegg got that chance. He was flying another plane load of rescue dogs to Kelley Curtis, and called before leaving

Alabama, to let her know when he would be on the ground in Tampa. Before hanging up, he asked how Eyelet was doing, and Curtis said, "I'll bring her out."

"The difference in that dog was amazing," says Clegg. "When I had last seen her she was almost dead from malnutrition and could barely walk, and here we are about eight months later, a whole new dog. She had body fat and was wagging her tail and walking around like a regular dog. It was really great to see the change. It makes you feel good."

Several months after the transport that helped save a mother dog and her pups (facing page), pilot Steve Clegg was reunited with Eyelet in Tampa, Florida.

PUPS ON
APPROACH

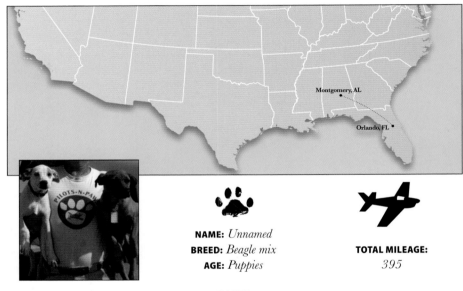

NAME: *Unnamed*
BREED: *Beagle mix*
AGE: *Puppies*

TOTAL MILEAGE:
395

ROUTE:
Montgomery, Alabama–Orlando, Florida

Some days, productivity just goes to the dogs. The personnel at Showalter Flying Service had no idea that the Cirrus SR22 landing at Orlando Executive Airport on a sultry August afternoon in 2009 would bring a bit of playful chaos to their day. But it didn't take long for word of the plane's unusual cargo to spread throughout the office. And when pilot Jeff Bennett opened the doors on thirteen beagle puppies being transported from central Alabama to no-kill animal rescues in central Florida, the people of Showalter knew just what to do—play!

"As soon as we saw those pups, everyone available jumped into action," recalls Brad Elliott, a Showalter director. Using aircraft tie-downs as makeshift leashes, Elliott and others wrangled the puppies and led them to a grassy area across the ramp for a

Top: PNP pilot Jeff Bennett off-loads two of thirteen pups in Orlando, Florida. Bottom: Showalter Flying Service employee Lauren Key enjoys a snuggle break with one of Bennett's passengers.

bit of relief and much-needed running around.

When the rescue volunteer scheduled to meet the plane was delayed, the offices of Showalter morphed into an impromptu doggie daycare as office employees, ground crew, and even customers enjoyed a joyous romp with the beagle baker's dozen.

"This was midafternoon and it was hot," remembers PNP pilot Bennett, "so there was no way I was going to keep thirteen dogs in the plane. Without me saying a word, all these people from the FBO [fixed base operator—in this case, Showalter] just came out and started helping—grabbing crates and puppies and taking them for walks. It was fantastic."

For the Alabama 13, it was a perfect way to kick off their reclaimed lives. Giving and getting love in equal measure, they left smiles and the story of a great day at the office in their wagging wake. Fantastic indeed.

Left: Showalter staff used aircraft tie-downs as makeshift leashes for their unexpected visitors. Right: Showalter's Brad Elliott enjoys the distraction.

A PILOT'S PILOT

Bremerton, WA · Seattle, WA

Olympia, WA

NAME: *Pilot*
BREED: *Australian shepherd*
AGE: *One year*

TOTAL MILEAGE:
86

ROUTE:
Seattle, Washington–Olympia, Washington
Olympia, Washington–Bremerton, Washington

If you want to get a job done, give it to a busy person—that's the old saw. Amateur pilot Robin Lee certainly qualifies. Lee holds down three jobs in her home city of Seattle—all of them in the aviation field. She's passionate about flying ("Some people get bit by the flying bug," she says. "I have a congenital case."), but her passions don't stop there. A lifelong animal lover, she frequently volunteers with local rescue operations for both horses and dogs.

Smart, working animals hold special appeal for Lee. "I guess that's why I like herding breeds," says Lee. "They like to have real work to do." For many years, Lee has volunteered as a representative with the Aussie Rescue and Placement Helpline—a nonprofit that helps place orphaned Australian shepherds into permanent homes. With two Aussies of her own at home, she understands the unique demands of the intelligent and energetic breed.

PNP pilot Robin Lee with the dog soon to be named Pilot in her honor.

"Most Australian shepherds would certainly be smart enough to help me operate in the cockpit," she jokes, "but the lack of opposable thumbs and ability to speak clearly to ATC [air traffic control] in English hinders their full potential as copilots."

In the spring of 2010, another helpline volunteer told Lee about a one-year-old deaf Aussie that had landed in an Olympia, Washington, animal shelter. This dog, she learned, was a "double merle," meaning it carried two copies of the merle gene (the gene that results in an Aussie's unusual merle pattern of bluish- or reddish-gray fur dotted with black). Double merles are usually hearing and/or visually impaired if not completely deaf and blind. "They are mostly white," says Lee. "They're stunning to look at, but even more difficult to place than 'normal' Aussies due to lack of suitable, knowledgeable homes. Many are culled at birth."

Knowing how difficult finding a suitable home for this dog could be, Lee got in touch with another member of the Pacific Northwest "Aussie network," a woman who ran a rescue called DART, Deaf Aussie Rescue and Training.

"She was willing to foster and work with our boy if we could get him up to her. She lives in a town called

Deming, which is on the Nooksack River, approximately twenty miles from the Canadian border. Olympia, where the pup was, is more than 150 miles to the south. By car, it is three or four hours, depending on traffic. It's doable, but the idea of a rambunctious, untrained adolescent who can't hear and possibly can't quite see being cooped up in a vehicle for that length of time was a bit daunting."

Lee suggested transporting him via PNP to shorten his journey. The request was posted to the PNP board, and she signed up for the mission. Knowing she might have her hands full, she invited another dog-loving pilot to fly along. They flew from Seattle to Olympia to pick up the passenger.

"When we taxied up to the FBO [fixed base operator], I could see our volunteer and a snow white Aussie pup waiting for us at a picnic table outside," remembers Lee. "She had him both on a harness and a collar, with a strong leash attached to each, because he was very bouncy and energetic and unable to hear his handler's voice. Although most dogs usually just settle down in the backseat of an airplane and go to sleep, I had some doubts when I saw the little hooked marlin on the ramp."

She need not have worried. The hum of the engine worked its magic on the rambunctious pup, and he stayed calm for the hour-long flight. Arriving at Bremerton National Airport, Lee delivered her new friend to a very grateful foster mom, who promptly christened the dog "Pilot."

Lee stayed in touch with Pilot's foster mom and delighted in reports that he had taken to his schooling "like a champ," and was not, as previously thought, entirely deaf. After a few months of basic training with the foster volunteer, Pilot was placed in his forever home. Lee—this time in her role as an Aussie rescue volunteer—conducted the adoption interview herself.

Pilot's adoptive mom, Stephanie Ogata, says the dog's strange eyes and unusual name both contributed to his appeal as they searched for a new dog. "No other dog caught our eye the way Pilot did," she says. She does admit, however, that once the adoption was final, she and her husband considered renaming him. "We threw a few names around, but none of them stuck like 'Pilot' did." She laughs, adding, "He now fits the name very well as we find him to constantly be looking at the sky and ceiling when he hears noises—and he's also a little 'flighty' and hyperactive . . . but we love him very much."

Robin Lee isn't surprised to hear that things are working out. "I had a good feeling about them, and I am thrilled for him," says Lee. "I'm glad he now has a chance at a better life . . . and that one pilot was able to help another."

Pilot now enjoys life at home in Dupont, Washington, with his new brother, Ziggy.

BOXER, UNDEFEATED

NAME: *Sully*
BREED: *Boxer*
AGE: *Two years*

TOTAL MILEAGE:
608

ROUTE:
Indianapolis, Indiana–Aurora, Illinois
Aurora, Illinois–Red Wing, Minnesota

May Heckman has never met the dog known to thousands as "Sully." But she'll never forget the day she first saw him. She had received an urgent text message and photo from a friend—a fellow boxer rescue volunteer in a large Midwestern city.

"I looked at that picture and said, 'What the hell is this,' you know?"

She sent the photo to her e-mail so she could get a better look. Then she responded to her colleague: "What on Earth . . . ?"

"He was brought into us today," came the reply.

"Oh, my God. Is he alive?"

"Barely."

That picture of Sully would have a similar jarring effect on the many people who would see it in the days and weeks to come—and it set off a heroic effort to save his life.

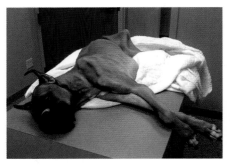

Sully had been starved nearly to death when this photo was taken at a vet clinic in December 2009.

"You couldn't look at that picture and not be moved."

—Pete Howell, PNP volunteer and Sully rescuer

As shocking as Sully's picture was, the story that led up to it was even more difficult to believe. The young male boxer had been abused by a man whose wife had left him. The dog, which had belonged to his wife but was left behind when she moved out, was starved out of spite. Vets who examined him after he was seized and placed in protective custody estimated that Sully was days, if not hours, away from death.

Minnesota Boxer Rescue agreed to take Sully in, but the critically neglected dog was six hundred miles away in Indiana. Heckman was certain he wouldn't survive ground transportation, so she turned to PNP for help. Two pilots, Mike Gerdes and Pete Howell, took up Sully's cause.

"When the boxer ladies put their mind to something, just get out of the way, because it's going to happen. You can either get on board the train or it's gonna run you over."

—Pete Howell, discussing the volunteers of Minnesota Boxer Rescue

Gerdes flew the first leg, meeting Sully's rescuers at a small airport in Indiana. He'd made his 1966 Piper Cherokee as comfortable as possible, fashioning a bed from pillows and blankets. "He was so weak I worried that we might break a bone by lifting him into the plane," Gerdes remembers. But the dog surprised him with his spirit. "He was very gentle and seemed to love the attention. Even in the bad shape he was in, you could look into his eyes and see that he was a sweetheart just looking for someone to care about him."

Gerdes flew at low altitude and cranked the heat in the old Cherokee to keep Sully as warm as possible. It was late December and the Midwestern skies were clear and

PNP pilots Mike Gerdes (left, with veterinarian Tara Harris) and Pete Howell (top) flew Sully over the frozen Midwest.

frigid. As he flew north, one hand repeatedly reached behind his seat to stroke and pat the large, gaunt dog. Within thirty minutes or so, Sully fell into a deep sleep.

A rendezvous was planned with Pete Howell in Aurora, Illinois, and "Pilot Pete" was right on time. Gerdes briefed Howell on Sully's condition, transferred the dog's paperwork, and helped load Sully into Howell's two-seater.

Sully's initial impression on Howell is indelible. "It was unbelievable," he remembers. "When I first saw the dog it was hard to believe what I was seeing. The transport coordinator had warned me that this was a bad case, so I was prepared, but it was just shocking. My dad was a vet, so I'd seen a lot, but I'd never seen anything like that before. Literally, everyone in the airport office just stopped and stared. Yet, this dog who clearly had been abused by people in all kinds of different ways . . . he was the nicest dog you'd ever want to meet. Very calm. Very friendly. It was something to see." This boxer was a fighter, that much was clear.

> **"Four or five minutes into the flight, he just stuck his big head on my lap, and at that point it was one of the better days I've had in a long time."**
>
> *—Pete Howell*

Sully meets foster mom Stephanie Murphy at the airport in Red Wing, Minnesota. Murphy would ultimately adopt him permanently.

Sully's arrival at a small airport in Red Wing, Minnesota, on the afternoon of December 29, 2009, was much anticipated. Waiting at the airport were the director of Minnesota Boxer Rescue, Valerie Current, and a foster volunteer, Stephanie Murphy. Murphy had agreed to take on the demanding job of caring for Sully during his long and intensive recovery. She already had three dogs at home, including a three-legged boxer she had adopted the previous year. She didn't intend to adopt Sully, but knew he would be with her for a while.

"When I first met him, I wanted to cry at his condition," remembers Murphy. "But he wouldn't allow me to, showering my face with kisses instead."

She worried about how her dogs would react to the emaciated hulk of a boxer. They had not always been welcoming to the dogs she'd fostered in the past. But those fears were put to rest on the first night. "They seemed to know that he needed companionship and warmth. My small dogs—a Jack Russell and a mini boxer—actually laid right on top of him to keep him warm."

Murphy began posting updates about Sully on YouTube, and hundreds of people around the country followed his progress as he slowly gained weight and energy. Minnesota Boxer Rescue also posted frequent Sully updates on its Web site. Watching the short video clips, one experiences a disconnect. Here is a nearly skeletal dog, barely able to walk just a few weeks earlier—but now romping, barking, and waggling his boney hindquarters like a puppy. This dog seems unaware of his condition, unfazed by having been so close to death. But a month after arriving in Minnesota, Sully's rooters received a blow. He was diagnosed with bone cancer and given two to five months to live. Murphy decided right then to officially adopt Sully and let him live out his remaining few months as part of a family.

But even as she watched her dog struggle with arthritis and a badly swollen leg, she marveled at his irrepressible spirit as he did his best to play with the other household dogs. She couldn't give up on him. Not yet. Murphy and the foster coordinator at MBR decided to get a second opinion. And with it, Sully got a reprieve. The bone cancer, they learned, had been misdiagnosed. Sully was suffering instead from a fungal disease, blastomycosis—still dire, but treatable.

Treatments are expensive—around $600 a month—and sometimes need to be continued for twelve months or more. Without help, says Murphy, "I'd be in way over my head." But Sully's spirit has won him a significant cheering section, and contributions have come in to ensure that he gets the antifungal treatments necessary to save his life—that is, to save his life *again*. One sponsor, who learned of Sully's story on MBR's Facebook page, donated $500 . . . then $500 more. A few months later, the man flew from Ohio just to meet his beneficiary. To date, the anonymous donor has paid nearly $5,000 for Sully's medical treatments. There's just something about this dog.

Sully is holding strong. The blastomycosis is stubborn and his immune system was left severely weakened by his long starvation. But the swelling is down in his leg. He still receives his medicine mixed into a peanut butter sandwich every morning. He still loves to romp and run with his canine housemates.

Most important, he still has the support, love, and prayers of the many people he has touched since his weary, drawn body was handed over to astonished caregivers in the waning days of 2009. This boxer has so many in his corner.

"People say I'm crazy to have taken this on," says Stephanie Murphy, "but I'm not going to give up on Sully. Three of my dogs are rescued—they've already had somebody give up on them."

It's been a long, tough fight, and there are still many rounds to go. But no one's counting Sully out.

> **"Sully's story demonstrated the best and the worst that people can be toward animals. It's an example of how caring, concerned people can take a suffering animal and turn its life around to bring joy to so many."**
>
> —*Mike Gerdes, PNP pilot*

Sully at home with his new forever family.

RUNT
TRIUMPHANT

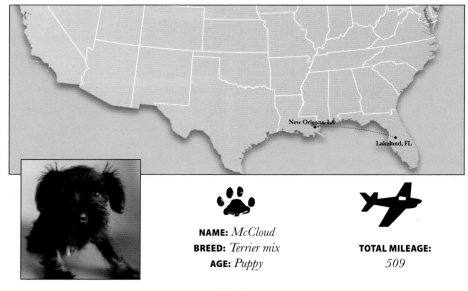

NAME: *McCloud*
BREED: *Terrier mix*
AGE: *Puppy*

TOTAL MILEAGE:
509

ROUTE:
New Orleans, Louisiana–Lakeland, Florida

The dogs of America's Gulf Coast have had a rough run of years. Hurricane Katrina left thousands of pets stranded or abandoned as families fled New Orleans and surrounding communities. Households struggling for financial survival were forced to make heartbreaking decisions, and countless dogs and cats were surrendered to animal shelters already swelling past capacity. The Gulf of Mexico oil rig disaster of 2010 only compounded problems as further economic hardship stressed Gulf Coast communities.

So when a cardboard box of wiggling weeks-old puppies was found alongside a busy street and turned into the St. John Parish Animal Shelter in LaPlace, Louisiana, in early September 2010, no one was terribly surprised—the litter joined the ever-growing ranks of the unclaimed. Animal abandonments like this were depressingly common in the parishes of Louisiana.

Lucky for these pups, they were young and adorable. Shelter workers knew they had a good chance at adoption—especially if they were moved to a more urban shelter. Jacob Stroman, shelter director at the nearby Plaquemines Animal Welfare Society (PAWS), offered to take the pups at his facility. They were transferred, cleaned up, and vetted, and within a few weeks, all were adopted out.

All except one.

While conducting a preliminary examination on the animals, Dr. Marcia Riedel of Furry Friends Animal Hospital noticed an unusual swelling on the abdomen of one of the pups. She could tell immediately that he had a hernia and sent him to a different animal hospital for further tests.

An ultrasound exam showed a thoracic wall hernia. The little dog's sternum had never completely fused, resulting in a smaller than normal thoracic cavity and an underdeveloped diaphragm. The surgical expertise to fix such a condition simply didn't exist locally, Dr. Riedel was told. "I was pretty disappointed," she says. "But the clinic employees and I agreed to keep him and try to find a special home for him." He might not live a full life, she knew, but she was determined to make the time he did have as happy as possible.

Throughout his ordeal, the little pup remained spirited and scrappy with a strong appetite—in other words, full of life. Maybe he knew something his doctors didn't, because though he'd been born with poor health, he did have very fortunate timing. At the very time he and his siblings were abandoned at the St. John shelter, final plans were coming together for a one-day intensive animal-rescue fly-in at nearby Lakefront Airport in New Orleans.

Jacob Stroman, director of PAWS, had been informed about the upcoming "life-flight" to Florida and asked to select some of the shelter's strays for transport. Suspecting that the little dog's prospects for surgery might improve in Florida, he consulted Dr. Riedel.

"I felt that it would be an excellent chance for him—if he could be accepted," says Dr. Riedel. "Not many rescue groups are willing to accept a surgical special-needs puppy. But as there didn't appear to be much, if any, chance of him being fixed here, we submitted him as a candidate."

Five hundred miles away, at the SPCA shelter in Lakeland, Florida, operations director Patt Glenn saw the little dog's picture and read his story. "I could not get him out of my mind," Glenn recalls. "I kept going back to him, not sure what to do, and then I thought, 'Well, if they think he's well enough to fly, then let's try.'" In her head, she began compiling a list of people who she could ask for donations to pay for his surgery.

Thus the little dog with the big medical problem joined the ranks of the lucky animals who would leave New Orleans on an autumn morning in 2010, bound for brighter futures.

Dr. Riedel cried when she said good-bye to the dog. She also decided to give him a name. She christened him "McCloud," taking the name from the 1986 movie *Highlander*. "It's spelled differently in the movie, but the character played by Christopher Lambert lived forever. This dog needed a good, strong name to protect him through his hopefully anticipated surgery."

On September 18, 2010, McCloud was one of 171 dogs flown out of New Orleans Lakefront Airport—seventy-nine of which were bound for Florida. His pilot and crew—Todd and Mary Brooks—loaded McCloud into their Cessna 182 along with eight other dogs.

Before departing, Stroman made them aware that they were carrying a special passenger.

"I vividly remember telling the pilots who were flying McCloud that he was born with a rare birth defect that they should know about," recalls Stroman. "I didn't want to scare them, but I felt that I had to tell them as his condition was pretty serious. I told them that there was a small chance that he could have problems with the excitement of the flight."

PNP volunteers Todd and Mary Brooks flew McCloud and eight other rescued dogs from New Orleans to Florida.

As it turns out, he needn't have worried. "McCloud made the trip with no problems," Mary Brooks reported in an online flight diary. "He slept the whole way." She added, "He was a very loving dog. We hope that he finds very special parents."

One week later, and just twenty days after being discovered abandoned in a cardboard box in Louisiana, McCloud underwent surgery to reconstruct his thoracic cavity and diaphragm at Veterinary Healthcare Associates (VHA) in Winter Haven, Florida. VHA veterinarian Dr. Alister Chapnick performed the complicated surgery at no cost. Scrappy little McCloud sailed through with no complications. His prognosis for a long, normal life is excellent.

If McCloud's story ended here, it would end happy enough, but this tale of redemption gets even better. While still recovering from surgery at VHA, McCloud caught the eye of another doctor making her rounds. Dr. Dawn Morgan-Winter fell hard for the scruffy little dog. When he was released from the hospital a few days later, she officially adopted him.

Receiving the update on McCloud back at his shelter in Plaquemines Parish, Louisiana, Jacob Stroman had to take a

After assisting with McCloud's medical care in Florida, Dr. Dawn Morgan-Winter decided to take him home.

moment in the midst of a typically hectic day to process what had just transpired.

"I just found out the good news," he e-mailed the collection of partisans that had all played a role in giving McCloud an unlikely second chance. "I am absolutely dumbfounded and blown away," he wrote. "We hoped for an appropriate home for McCloud, but holy smokes—this is just plain unbelievable!"

"I really believe there was a reason for all of us to be touched by McCloud. There were too many obstacles he overcame, and so many people believing in him along the way not to."

—*Patt Glenn, operations director, Lakeland SPCA, Lakeland, Florida*

UP IN THE AIR
WITH UNCLE JIM

Knoxville, TN

If you ask Tennessee-based pilot Jim Carney to share a few of his favorite rescue flight stories, you'd best pull up a chair and get comfortable. Carney has flown hundreds of animals to safety since his first Pilots N Paws flight in the spring of 2009—around two hundred in the year 2010 alone—and he finds something to love about almost all of them.

That love shines through in the photographs he shoots during every mission. "Most of my pictures of my dog passengers are taken in-flight," says Carney. "That way I can record their expressions of flying. You can get some really unique shots." One of his favorites is of a very pregnant Doberman lying serenely on his plane's backseat. Just a few days after that flight, the dog gave birth to nine pups. That timely transport earned him the nickname "Uncle Jim" from a group of Doberman rescuers.

"Posed pictures on the ground always look the same. I like to capture the dogs' expressions while flying."

Carney can conjure up stories from dozens of his rescue flights—little details about the canine passengers or the ground-based volunteers who he contends do most of the "real" work. His memory is assisted by scrapbooks filled with flight records and at least a few photos from every flight.

Like virtually all pilots who volunteer with PNP, Carney has the twin passions requisite for the job: "I love animals and I love flying airplanes," he says. "So Pilots N Paws was a natural. After retiring as a 747 captain for Northwest Airlines in 2004, I realized that aviation had been very good to me," says Carney. "I knew it was payback time." Carney credits PNP with giving him extra incentive to get back up in the air.

Carney's rescue flights have taken him as far afield as California, but his bread and butter is regional flights—generally east and northeast from Tennessee. Whenever prudent, he likes his passengers to ride in the backseat—unkenneled but tethered to the seat frame by a leash. "That way they can't jump up and help me fly the airplane . . . which happened once," he says, teasing in yet another in-flight tale. "But it turned out all right." With the plane's autopilot on, Carney relishes every opportunity to interact with his passengers. "I've always got my arm back there petting them," he says. "It makes me feel so good to look back and watch them. I do feel they know something good will come out of what is happening to them, as if they have a soul.

"When you're helping a dog get to a new home, you are also helping the new or soon-to-be adoptive family get their new pet—it becomes a win-win. A life saved, happiness gained. I can't think of a better reward for helping."

PILOT SAM GETS A FEW POINTERS

Sioux Falls, SD

Leavenworth, KS

Eureka, KS

Roanoke, TX

NAME: *"The Wild Bunch"*
BREED: *German shorthaired pointers*
AGE: *Assorted*

TOTAL MILEAGE:
1,039

ROUTE:
Leavenworth, Kansas–Sioux Falls, South Dakota
Sioux Falls, South Dakota–Eureka, Kansas
Eureka, Kansas–Roanoke, Texas

Shortly after flying his first rescue mission for Pilots N Paws in the spring of 2009, Kansas City–based pilot Sam Taylor had an idea. He shopped around online and found a small decal sticker— a silhouette of a dog. He stuck it to the side of his plane to commemorate the successful mission. One dog, one sticker.

Sam Taylor applies another decal.

The stickers started adding up quickly in the months that followed. Row after row of dog silhouettes were added to the side of his 1964 Piper Cherokee as Sam's name quickly became known to transport coordinators looking to move dogs through the middle of the country.

There's a story behind every sticker on Taylor's plane. One of Sam's favorites is best told in his own words:

I saw a call for moving five German shorthaired pointer dogs from Sioux Falls, South Dakota, southward on the Pilots N Paws Web site. I had never moved five adult uncrated dogs at one time before, but I figured I could fit them all in if I removed the rear seat of my plane. So I made the modifications and contacted the rescue coordinator and headed out, curious to see how they would all fit and how they'd get along.

On the ground in Sioux Falls, the rescue staff began escorting the five GSPs to me. They looked like very nice dogs. I figured I'd put them in the rear of the plane and in about two hours I'd transfer them to the next two pilots taking them on to Texas. I secured their leashes to tie-downs I had in the floorboards, which enabled them to stand and walk around a bit, but not interfere with me as I flew the plane.

The dogs were all brought aboard without incident. I started the engine and taxied to the active runway. I took off and then leveled off at a VFR [visual flight rules] cruising altitude.

One dog in particular began to become agitated. He looked around as if to say, "What the heck's going on here?" and began to bark. Others arose to the beckoning, and I could see things were beginning to get out of control. I grabbed the unruly dog by the collar and yelled, "Knock it off!" It seemed to

A brief moment of calm during an action-packed flight. (Note dog slobber on pilot's shoulder.)

work for a while. Then I noticed the dogs began to drool. This normally is an indication that the dogs are getting airsick. Soon they were vomiting and then defecating. Not a pleasant experience when you're in an enclosed compartment a few thousand feet above the ground with little ability to vent the air.

There is a commonly held rule among rescue animal transport people that you do not feed or water a rescue animal on the day it is being transported. Unfortunately, this totally contradicts one of our established American cultural courtesies. When guests leave your home, the last thing you do is give them a big meal. Most of the time, that's a nice gesture; with rescue animals, not so much. Apparently this rescue did not know about the "Do not feed" protocol, and I was paying the price.

With the somewhat loose leashes the five dogs were able to walk around and step in the vomit and in the poop and then on me. In short order—and with a couple of flight hours still to go—I was quite noticeably "marked" as belonging to this group.

One friendly dog, through no fault of her own a member of this unruly group, came to me as I was flying and put her head on my shoulder. I snapped a photo of her and that photo has become one of my favorites. The poor dog had a look of, "What is going to happen to us?" These dogs had just come out of a rough situation, and most certainly had no idea where they were going, so I understood her worried look.

Eureka, Kansas (sorry, Eurekans), is in the middle of nowhere. It was our predestined rendezvous airport because it was on the route and had good fuel prices. I landed and was looking forward to passing these dogs on, getting rid of the stench, and washing up. After taxiing off the runway and onto the ramp, I opened the door on my Piper Cherokee. One of the dogs, unbeknownst to me, had gotten out of her harness and was cleverly waiting at the rear of the plane for her chance to bolt. When the door opened, out she went. She jumped off the wing, darted off the ramp, paralleled the runway for a couple hundred feet, then veered off onto the prairie.

I quickly unbuckled my seat belt and ran after her. Looming in the back of my mind was the admittedly selfish thought "There goes my perfect record of having never lost an animal in transit."

I called for her, pleaded for her to return, and offered her treats and water, but she would have none of it. Then the airport manager, Larry Dutton, came out on a noisy riding lawn mower and asked me if I needed any help. I explained the situation and pointed to the little shrinking brown-and-white dot off in the distance. He looked in the direction of the dog and then at me and said, "I'll go get her." I went back to the plane and untied the remaining dogs and brought them out of the plane and tied them to a post in a shaded area. Then I went into the airport manager's office to cool down and to begin the process of exchanging the animals with the next pilots.

PNP pilot John Watson took two of the wild bunch on a second-leg flight to Roanoke, Texas.

Next thing I knew, here's the dog resting on the lawn mower as the manager drives—clankety-clank—into the ramp area. All I could do was say, "Thank you for keeping my record of never losing a dog intact." Apparently the dog had a strong desire to run to its freedom, but just did not have the strength. When Larry had gotten to her, she was lying down and panting and put up no resistance as he gently lifted her onto the mower.

She was too tired to walk, so I carried her into a small enclosed area of the hangar next to the manager's office. I laid her on the floor and gave her a bowl of water and left her there to rest. I went into the office and completed the paperwork for the exchange and then went to get her.

She was gone. I quickly searched throughout the hangar. I was certain she had found a way out and had fled again, this time for good. There was quite a bit of machinery in the hangar so I began looking under and behind things. There she was, lying under some equipment. Poor dog just wanted to be left alone for a while, but she had to move on. Once she made it through this day, her life would greatly improve. I carried her to the next pilot.

I gave her and another dog to John Watson, who had flown up out of Addison, Texas, and three to George Schwab, from Denton, Texas. We bid our farewells, then I located a bucket of warm, soapy water and began the task of cleaning out my airplane. Once the plane was clean, I washed up as best I could, and flew back to Kansas City.

Another mission accomplished for pilot Sam Taylor—and another five *very hard earned* decals for the well-traveled Piper Cherokee.

Postscript

by Sam Taylor

The second "layer" of this story is the rescue flight coordination conducted by Elizabeth ("Liza") Bondarek of Cape Cod, Massachusetts, which resulted in thirty-seven GSPs being flown out of South Dakota.

Liza is a cook at a restaurant on the cape by day, and the rest of the time she is a volunteer with GSP Rescue New England. She is one of many stalwart rescue coordinators who spend countless hours behind the scenes doing the nerve-wracking work of setting up multileg rescues. She tells me it is not uncommon for her, after hours of coordinating a flight to meet the pilots' capabilities and comfort zones, distances willing to fly, all the "what if" questions and so on, to get a call on the day of execution: "My plane won't start." But she somehow makes it happen, primarily because she has educated herself in the art and science of general aviation. General aviation—the flying in and out of the hundreds of small, uncontrolled airfields throughout the United States—is a world of its own, with its own culture, language, and codes. Liza understands this world and can communicate with pilots, which makes the transports go smoothly and efficiently.

When the need to find homes and transportation for forty-two German shorthaired pointers came to the attention of the National German Shorthair Pointer Rescue's headquarters, it immediately went to Liza for help. She took on this daunting task and over the next several months flew thirty-seven of them out through Pilots N Paws. The others went by land transport.

I have worked with Liza on several GSP rescues, and over the months we have developed a friendly rapport and a mutual respect. When I call her, I introduce myself by saying, "Is this mission control?" and she responds, "Is this my favorite pilot?" to which I respond, "You say that to all the pilots."

Liza Bondarek's hound, Siegfried, monitors the computer at "Mission Control" in Cape Cod, Massachusetts.

HELL ON WHEELS

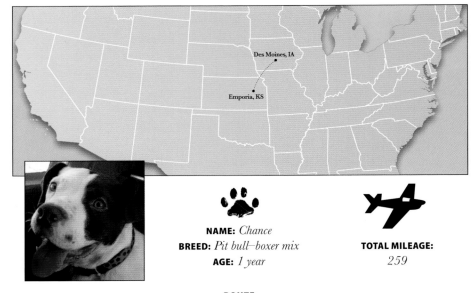

NAME: *Chance*
BREED: *Pit bull–boxer mix*
AGE: *1 year*

TOTAL MILEAGE:
259

ROUTE:
Emporia, Kansas–Des Moines, Iowa

Steel wheels rolled down the railroad track into the heart of Emporia, a city of twenty-five thousand on the upland prairie of eastern Kansas. Whether the engineer ever saw the dog on the track isn't known. But someone witnessed the horrific incident and made an emergency call. To call it an accident wouldn't be quite right. Sheriff's department personnel who investigated the scene would later tell attending veterinarians that the dog wasn't on the track by accident. Someone had put him there—and restrained him so he couldn't escape those rolling steel wheels. An eastbound freight train clipped his hind end. When the impact of that strike spun him around, a westbound train hit his head.

Animal Control officers collected the pit bull–boxer mix off the side of the tracks and took him to a nearby vet clinic. No one expected him to survive the night. But when the clinic opened in the morning, they were met with a surprise. The dog, though battered, bloody, and unable to walk, was not just alive, but alert.

Christina ("Tina") Khan teaches English as a second language in Topeka, about an hour northeast of Emporia, but around Emporia, she's better known for her avocation than her vocation. As vice president of a nonprofit animal-welfare group in Emporia, Khan's the woman area animal shelters and vets call with hard-luck cases. This one certainly qualified.

By the time Khan got word of the critically injured dog, he had already been bandaged up and sent to the city animal shelter. "The city wasn't going to pay for vetting or critical care," she explains.

Khan and another rescue volunteer intervened. They hustled to the shelter to pick up the dog and take him back to the vet. On the way, they struck a quick bargain. The other volunteer, Karen Todd, would pay for the dog's vetting, and Tina Khan would foster and rehabilitate the dog after it was patched up.

Khan wasn't sure what to expect at the shelter. The shelter manager had already told her that the dog should probably be put to sleep. Even without a full vet exam, it was obvious that his back legs were at least partially paralyzed.

Khan arrived to find a dog broken in body but bursting with spirit. "We walked in and he was just like, 'Hi, guys! How's it going?' I mean, here was this dog dragging himself around—couldn't move anything other than his front end—but just high energy, grinning and panting, with his ears up. He had such a spirit."

She and Todd drove the dog back to the vet clinic, where, despite the patient's fighting spirit, they received the same unwelcome advice—put the dog to sleep. "I said, 'Absolutely not,'" recalls Khan. "Not an option. We're not going to euthanize him because he's paralyzed. He'll be a wonderful, adoptable dog. To survive something like that . . . my God, if he survived trying to be eliminated by a train, who am I to not give him a chance?"

Three days of care later—including treatment of a cracked skull, sinus blood clots, multiple cuts and scrapes on his head, neck, and face, and a full exam of his nonworking hindquarters, the dog was ready for release. Khan was there to pick him up and take him home. Up

Rescuer Tina Khan says good-bye to Chance in Gardner, Kansas.

until then, he had been referred to simply as "the train dog." Khan signed him out of the clinic as "Chance." "He didn't need to be reminded of that," she says.

Chance spent several weeks in Khan's home, where he was made welcome by her four resident dogs. His condition steadily improved, and he kept up surprisingly well, pulling himself by his muscular upper body, dragging his back legs behind. But Khan knew he needed a home where he could receive more care and therapy—and she needed to free up her foster space for other hard-luck cases at the shelter—so after two months or so, she started looking to place Chance in a forever home.

This is the story of three determined women, two caring pilots, and one incredibly tough dog. The second woman in the story lives in Adel, Iowa, some three hundred miles from Tina Khan's home in Kansas. The two have never met personally, but they are kindred spirits in the sense that they each dedicate a large percentage of their waking hours (and disposable income) to help dogs in need.

Amy Heinz is the founder and president of AHeinz57 Pet Rescue and Transport, located about thirty miles west of Des Moines. Heinz got into the animal-transport "business" accidentally about five years ago after volunteering to drive two homeless rat terriers from her local shelter to an animal rescue in Minneapolis. Since that time, her organization—like Khan's, a 501(c)(3) registered charity with an all-volunteer staff—has become a vital link in the transport network that moves rescue animals across the country. "Because of our location, we're actually a hub of transport," she says. "Dogs go east and west and north and south, and I-35 and I-80 intersect right here." Little did she know when she moved from California to Iowa in 2005 that she'd wind up right in the middle of things.

Heinz, a single mother, runs her expanding operation from her home on a small acreage. In the early years, she used her garage as a kennel. While animal transport has always been her primary objective, there are invariably those dogs that need a temporary home until a permanent one can be located. She's built a network of thirty families who actively participate in fostering dogs, and she recently leased a vacant vet clinic and set up a short-term boarding facility called "The Pit Stop." Her goal is to make the dogs feel as much "at home" as possible—it's furnished with comfy chairs and couches for the canine tenants. "We even have slumber parties there," says Heinz. "We spend the night and watch movies." It's not as frivolous as it may sound. "They'll make better dogs when they're adopted if they know what it's like to be in a home," she explains.

Amy Heinz had first met Tina Kahn a few weeks before when the former helped the latter transport and place another injured dog—also hit by a train in Emporia. That dog, nicknamed Joe Boxer, went on to be fostered and ultimately adopted by one of Heinz's foster families.

When Kahn began looking for a home for Chance, Amy Heinz was at the top of her list. "I called Amy and said, 'I've got this guy and he's going to need a really special home,'" says Kahn. "He's going to need a lot of attention."

"We couldn't take him into our foster system because I didn't have anyone who was home during the day," says Heinz. "But I told Tina I'd help her find a place for him. So I started sending out mass e-mails and crossposting everyone I knew."

Enter determined woman number three. Sara Henderson is cofounder and current president of the Pet Project Midwest, a Des Moines–based nonprofit with the mission of keeping pets with the people who love them. The organization's two main endeavors are a pet "food bank" for low-income animal owners and the creation and operation of Iowa Pet Alert, a Web- and mobile-based forum for reconnecting owners with missing pets.

When Henderson received the post about Chance from Heinz, she dutifully crossposted it to her own network, as she had with so many pet alerts in the past. But she couldn't quite get this one out of her head. It was the picture, more than anything, that got to her. "He had these ears that kind of flip forward and cover one of his eyes in the most adorable way," she recalls. "I kept looking at that picture, and every time I saw it I fell a little more in love. By the end of the second day, I thought, 'You're coming to my house to live.'"

Though it sounds like a wholly emotional decision, Henderson did conduct considerable due diligence before committing. She had long conversations with Khan to learn as much as she could about Chance's condition and prognosis. She sought out advice and input from other owners of handicapped pets. She spent hours on the Web site handicappedpets.com and thoroughly researched "Walkin' Wheels" and other dog "wheelchairs." She knew caring for Chance wouldn't be easy or cheap, but still . . . she knew—or at least felt fairly sure—that it was meant to be.

Her biggest concern was her home—an older house that she knew would be problematic for a dog with mobility issues. The biggest problem was an oversized kitchen island that left little clearance for a dog on wheels. That problem was solved in a single day when sixteen friends showed up, tore out her kitchen, and remodeled it sans island and built a ramp off her deck. "I have some seriously good friends," Henderson says.

In the meantime, Amy Heinz had gone into transport mode, reaching out to a handful of her tried-and-true Pilots N Paws volunteers. Kansas City–area pilot Jim Bordoni signed on for the transport. Knowing that the disabled dog would need extra care, he asked another KC-area PNP pilot, Sarah Owens, to fly along. A few days later, the two drove to Gardner, Kansas, where Bordoni hangars his Piper Cherokee and where they were met by Henderson and Chance.

"I expected to see a beaten-down, sad, scared, and pitiful creature," remembers Bordoni. "Boy, was I wrong! Chance may not have the use of his back legs, but it has not affected his spirit in the least. He may be one of the most loving and alert little guys I have ever transported." Bordoni had made a bed for Chance in the back of his plane, but Chance wasn't about to miss out on this once-in-a-lifetime experience. He sat up and looked out the window all the way to Des Moines.

Once on the ground in Iowa, Owens went into the fixed base operator to see if Heinz had arrived yet to meet them. "While Sarah was inside, I told the ramp guy Chance's story," says Bordoni. "The next thing you know, he had a baggage cart there to wheel Chance into the FBO." Owens rode along to keep Chance company.

Amy Heinz greeted the two pilots and their much-anticipated passenger and packed Chance up in her car for the last leg of his journey. At Sara Henderson's freshly renovated house, his new Walkin' Wheels and his very excited adoptive mother awaited.

A few months into his new life, Chance is thriving. Henderson, like everyone else who's met him along the way, marvels at his spirit. "He's just happy to be alive," she says. "He's smart, funny, and loyal as heck and doesn't have a clue that he's not perfect in every way."

Chance is already a fixture in the neighborhood doggie playgroup and took to his new wheels like a champ. "He loves playing with other dogs, and the wheels put him on more of a par with them," says Henderson. "When he gets tired he just plops down. His upper body goes into a lay, and his back legs hang from the wheels, and he's a happy kid."

Medical tests indicate that Chance does retain a small amount of mobility in his back legs, and Henderson has started him on physical therapy in hopes that he can regain some use of his hindquarters. "We're not sure where it will go," she says, "and he's absolutely fine as he is, but if we can get him more use of his legs, we're certainly going to try."

Top: Chance deplanes in Iowa. Bottom: PNP pilot Sarah Owens and Chance catch a ride to the fixed base operator on a baggage cart.

With his wheels on, Chance more than holds his own in the neighborhood playgroup. "You could never convince him he's not perfectly normal," says new mom Sara Henderson.

As the mother of a special-needs pet, Henderson has a message for others who might be considering adopting. "I want other people to be able to consider an animal like him and not think, 'Oh no, that's too much.' I realize it's not for everybody, but honestly after the first week, the benefits are so much more than any of the challenges. It's not the big drama I expected it to be."

"I'm just so grateful to PNP. They are such an awesome organization and have such dedicated people. They truly are angels to us down here on the ground."

—*Amy Heinz, AHeinz57 Pet Rescue and Transport*

"We pilots are just the taxicab. The real heroes are the rescues and fosters who devote their endless time and resources to save these deserving dogs."

—*Jim Bordoni, PNP pilot*

PRESTON

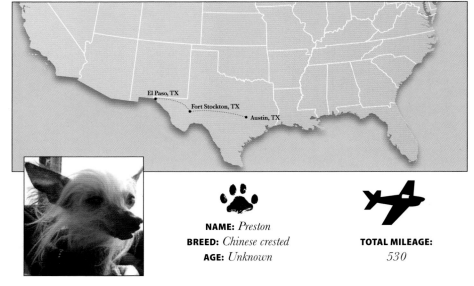

El Paso, TX
Fort Stockton, TX
Austin, TX

NAME: *Preston*
BREED: *Chinese crested*
AGE: *Unknown*

TOTAL MILEAGE:
530

ROUTE:
El Paso, Texas–Fort Stockton, Texas
Fort Stockton, Texas–Austin, Texas

Animal-rescue pilots hate to deadhead home, so PNP pilot Denise Pride was doubly happy to coordinate a two-way transport through central Texas in March 2010. She flew Wendy, a deaf poodle, from Austin to Fort Stockton, as one leg of a transport to the dog's new forever home in New Mexico. In Fort Stockton, she met up with another PNP pilot and swapped Wendy for two small dogs, a Japanese Chin on his way to an adoptive home in the Northeast, and a Chinese crested headed for a rescue in Austin.

In their short time together, the pint-sized Chinese crested, named Preston, claimed an outsized piece of Pride's heart. "He had been seized in an animal cruelty case," she says. "He had long nails, poor skin, wild hair, and no teeth, but was still the most loving dog one could ever meet. I fell instantly in love with the little guy."

Whether it's an "against all odds" survival story or simply the soulful look in their eyes, some animals just seem to touch humans a little more deeply. Tom Navar, MD, was the pilot who handed Preston off to Pride in Fort Stockton. He had flown from El Paso, while his wife, Tracy, held the little dog in her lap. The flight had been Navar's first as a PNP volunteer. In a postflight message to the others involved in Preston's successful transport, the deep impact it had on him was clear.

I had never flown animal rescues of any type before, but I wish to tell you how much I enjoyed meeting and working with you. Most of my flights are with cancer victims who need to be transported to treatment and are economically deprived. The most important thing I wish to share with you is that, even though I am not (in contrast to my wife and daughter) a dog person, I was, and will for a long time to come, be haunted by the look in the Chinese crested's eyes as he gazed at Tracy's face while she gently held him during the flight. There was no doubt that the dog was expressing its absolute trust, love, and appreciation for those around it that were helping him. The wisdom in the gaze of this venerable, profound creature spoke of a centuries-old bond with man. This was a life-changing experience, and I wish to thank you sincerely for allowing us to participate in it.

Preston with his Texas transport team. Above (from left): Dr. Tom Navar, Denise Pride, Reni Moczygemba, Tracy Estes Navar, and Maya Cameron Navar. Right: Preston with PNP pilot Denise Pride.

PHOENIX RISING

NAME: *Phoenix*
BREED: *Doberman*
AGE: *Five years*

TOTAL MILEAGE:
650

ROUTE:
Meridian, Mississippi–Tupelo, Mississippi*
Tupelo, Mississippi–Lancaster, Ohio

Years of abuse at the hands of her owners finally ended in outright abandonment. Neighbors say that when the family moved away, they literally threw the five-year-old Doberman out of the car on the outskirts of Meridian, Mississippi. A tough life seemed destined for a tragic end.

The dog survived that final heartless act as she had so many before, and eventually made her way back to the only home she'd known. Desperation brought her back—not happy memories. Multiple scars and a profound fear of people would attest to that. It was here that her owners had docked her ears and cropped her tail when she was just a pup—a home job with a sharp blade and no anesthesia. She'd dropped a litter of pups a year or so before—eleven in all. None survived past eight weeks. As she

* Ground (car) transport leg

wandered the woods near her former home, her belly had already started to swell with another litter. Neighbors threatened to shoot the dog if it kept showing up on their property. Never was a soul in more need of an angel.

In the summer of 2009, Suzanne Bruner was a college student living with her grandparents near the dog's former home. She first saw the forsaken dog while collecting eggs from a neighbor's chicken coop. She listened, horrified, as the neighbor related the dog's sorry story. She learned that it had been more than a month since its owners had moved on. The dog watched warily from the edge of the woods. Even from a distance, Bruner could see that it was emaciated and covered with cuts and contusions, including a broad patch of completely raw "road rash" across its side and hind leg.

In the rural community where opinions about the "nuisance" dog ran from chilly indifference to outright disdain, Suzanne felt something else: compassion. The dog wouldn't come to her, but she approached her slowly, quietly reassuring her. "Have you ever seen a dog in complete shut-down mode?" she asks. "Crouched down, shaking, absolutely terrified. . . ."

Eventually, the dog let Bruner near. The young woman picked her up and put her into her aunt's car. "Honestly, I didn't have a game plan," she says. "I just knew I had to get her out of there."

Once home, she tied the dog to a rusty horse trailer in the shade of a tree in her grandparents' yard. Her grandfather may have admired his granddaughter's heart, but he wasn't willing to let the dog stay permanently or to come inside the house.

For the next few weeks, Bruner tended to the dog the best she could. She fed her and tried to keep her wounds clean while they healed. She removed more ticks than she could count. Her means were limited, so mostly she worked on the dog's fragile emotional state. "I worked to get her where she wasn't so nervous around people," Bruner says. She also gave the dog a name. In optimistic anticipation of the new life she imagined for her, she christened the dog "Phoenix."

Bruner had suspected early on that Phoenix was pregnant. As the weeks went by, she became sure. She knew in her heart that the dog she had grown to love needed more help than she could provide.

She tried a nearby Doberman rescue first but they couldn't take Phoenix.

> "If there had been any way possible, I would have done anything to keep Phoenix. But I'm a college student. I work and live with someone who will not allow dogs in the house. She needed to be inside . . . with a family."
>
> —*Suzanne Bruner*

Through Internet posts she cast a wider net. Eventually, her desperate plea reached Alla McGeary, a volunteer with the Doberman Assistance Network (DAN) based in Winchester, Virginia.

Learning that the dog was pregnant but not knowing how far along, McGeary told Suzanne that they would need to act fast. "Get the dog cleaned up and get it a collar," she told Suzanne, then the experienced rescue coordinator set to work finding the dog a foster home.

McGeary worked her contact list hard. When various rescue groups hedged on whether they could take the dog or not, she admits to being curt. "My response was, 'I need an answer *now*—if we don't move on this, she is gonna have puppies under the tree.'"

Teka Clark of Northcoast Doberman Rescue, a small, independent rescue in Lancaster, Ohio, answered McGeary's call. "I can take her," said Clark. "Just get her here fast."

McGeary had plenty of experience with PNP animal transports. Now that she had a flight path—from eastern Mississippi to central Ohio—she set to work looking for pilots. The first to sign on for a transport leg was a man familiar to animal rescues in the Southeast—pilot Jim Carney, one of PNP's most prolific animal movers. When the urgency of the mission made finding additional pilots difficult, Carney told McGeary that if she could get the dog to Tupelo, he would fly her all the way to Teka Clark in Ohio.

Suzanne Bruner was amazed at how quickly things happened once McGeary took on Phoenix's cause. The student had never heard of Pilots N Paws before. When she learned from McGeary that Phoenix would be flying on a private plane from Mississippi to Ohio, she was flat-out astonished. "I thought that was the most awesome thing I'd ever heard," she says.

"I'm very happy that she found someone who was actually worthy of her. It kind of killed me a little to give her up because she was the most amazing dog I've ever known."

—*Suzanne Bruner*

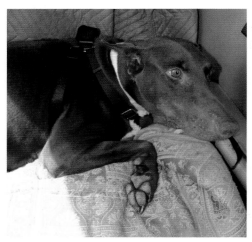

Pilot Jim Carney flew the very pregnant Phoenix all the way from Tupelo, Mississippi, to Ohio.

With little time to spare, the flight came off just three days later. Phoenix had started producing milk—usually a sign that whelping would occur within a week. Suzanne and her grandfather drove the dog two hours to Tupelo where they met rescue volunteer Kerry Panell. Panell kept Phoenix overnight and drove her to the airport the next morning in time to meet Carney, who had flown in from his home airport in Tennessee.

"Jim's only concern was, 'Are you sure she won't be delivering while I'm flying?'" says McGeary with a laugh. "Of course, we had no way of knowing for sure, but thought—and hoped—we still had a day or two." The flight, according to Carney, "was a nonevent." In pilot-speak, that's a good thing. For all she'd been through, Phoenix handled the unusual circumstances with aplomb, easily settling into the backseat of Carney's plane. "I'd reach back and pet her, and she would just kind of melt in my hand back there," Carney remembers. "She would just very gently touch my hand with her nose or give a little soft lick, like she was saying, 'Thanks for getting me out of that mess.'"

"It's quite a feeling to see the plane land and the dogs come off. They're so excited and the pilots are all grinning. . . . It's so much easier on the dogs, so less stressful. It's an amazing, wonderful program."

—*Teka Clark, Northcoast Doberman Rescue*

Safe on the ground in Ohio (pictured with Teka Clark and Angie Austin), Phoenix delivered nine healthy pups a few days later.

A few days after arriving at Clark's rescue, Phoenix delivered nine puppies—"all healthy and happy and good," she reported to Phoenix's growing list of supporters. After the pups were weaned, Phoenix started on heartworm meds, and Clark posted the pups and their mother on her site—available for adoption. The progeny of Phoenix now enjoy comfortable lives in Chicago, Virginia, Baltimore, Michigan, and Ohio. "People read about their mom on our Web site," says Clark, "and everybody wanted a Phoenix puppy."

Adopting out adorable puppies is generally not a problem. Placing a six-year-old heartworms survivor with a checkered past is more of a challenge. Clark received some inquiries, but she had a particular type of home in mind for this special dog. "We waited for the right match," she says, "and after about six weeks, we hit the jackpot."

Phoenix and Kate—two cast-off animals who have become constant companions at their new home in upstate New York.

A woman named Roxie put in an application. She lived on a horse farm in upstate New York with another rescued dog and several miniature ponies—also rescued. She'd read Phoenix's story and been touched. She'd seen Phoenix's picture and fallen in love.

Teka Clark arranged for a rescue colleague to make a site visit to the prospective adoptive home to assess its suitability. It was just as ideal as it sounded.

A few weeks later, Phoenix's new mom, Roxie, drove from New York to Ohio to claim her new forever dog. Now, as unlikely as it sounds, the dog once tied to a rusty horse trailer in rural Mississippi—abandoned, pregnant, and terrified—has acres to roam and, yes, a pony of her own. Phoenix has indeed risen, ably assisted by a host of angels.

> **"The PNP pilots are unbelievable. Every single time I've had pilots move a dog, they have bent over backward to help. I've had these guys fly at the drop of a hat to move these dogs. I've had them volunteer to hold dogs if we couldn't coordinate something with another pilot to come in. I can't say enough about them. They're animal people, and they are unbelievable."**
>
> —*Alla McGeary, rescue coordinator*

A MOVING STORY

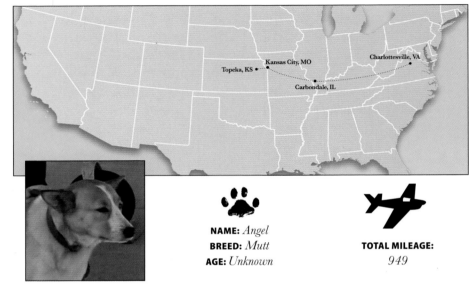

NAME: *Angel*
BREED: *Mutt*
AGE: *Unknown*

TOTAL MILEAGE:
949

ROUTE:
Topeka, Kansas–Kansas City, Missouri
Kansas City, Missouri–Carbondale, Illinois
Carbondale, Illinois–Charlottesville, Virginia

Kansas-based pilot Sarah Owens flew her first PNP passenger—a cat named Seymour—in early 2009. "After that trip," she says, "I was hooked! Pilots N Paws has become an addiction. I absolutely love it!"

Owens has flown around twenty missions since then, each with its own rewards and its own story. One of her favorites involved a family in need and a cross-country move.

In April 2009, I saw a post on the PNP Web site from a family in Marysville, Kansas. They were on a very tight budget and had to move to Virginia. They did not drive and would have to move via Greyhound. They could not afford to pay for transportation for their dog, Angel, and desperately wanted to take her with them.

It just happened that I was planning another PNP flight with another pilot, Karen, who offered to take Angel east, toward Virginia, after our previously scheduled flight. I offered to fly to Topeka and pick up Angel. When I got to Topeka, I met Angel's owners, who seemed very nervous about my "little airplane." I think they were skeptical that this thing would actually fly.

George, Angel's owner, was trying to be very stoic, but I could tell that this was hard for him, having to release his dog to a stranger and trust that everything would work out for transportation all the way to Virginia.

After some good-byes, I asked George and his wife, Cari, to help me load Angel in the plane. At this time, he just lost it. This man was so emotional about losing his dog, it just killed me. Good thing I was wearing sunglasses, because he was turning me into mush! I was practically a bawling baby as I taxied for takeoff—trying to hide my sniffles between communications with the air traffic control tower. I promised to take care of their precious cargo and call them as soon as we got to Kansas City, where I would be fostering the dog for one night, before its next flight. The flight was uneventful, and Angel was a great passenger. The next day, she flew with Karen, and made it back to George in Virginia within a few days. He was so thankful and sent me a very nice e-mail with pictures. It was such a great feeling to know that I was able to reunite this family."

Kansas-based PNP pilot Sarah Owens with Angel.

ALL SPECIES
AIRWAYS

Marathon, FL

The vast majority of animals rescued with the assistance of Pilots N Paws are dogs, but it's not unusual for pilots to transport cats now and then, and the odd rabbit occasionally benefits from PNP air transport, as well.

But as far as species variety is concerned, it's unlikely that any PNP pilot could match the collective flight manifest of Key West–based pilot Jeff Bennett.

In his first two years of flying PNP missions, Bennett has earned a reputation for being up for just about anything. Among the more than five hundred animals he's flown, there have certainly been dogs—lots of dogs (he's flown as many as twenty-three at a time in his Cirrus SR22)—but also rabbits, rats, guinea pigs, iguanas, a pot-bellied pig named Mo, and several very large snakes. Burmese pythons are something of a specialty.

"No one wants to fly snakes," the genial Bennett says incredulously. "I love to fly them! They're cold-blooded, and it gets hot in the plane, so you've got this great neck cooler, and they've got a warm rock to curl up around."

Self-deprecation is default mode for Bennett, so it's no surprise that he refers to his head as a warm rock. He's also frank, as many PNP pilots are, about the service they provide. "We [pilots] get a lot of notoriety for flying the dogs, but I gotta tell you, I'm just the bus," he says. "We get these animals after they've already been taken care of and nursed back to health. What the rescue volunteers and people on the ground deal with is the real work—their commitment and passion are just unbelievable."

Among the menagerie flown by PNP pilot Jeff Bennett, one of his favorite passengers was Mo, the pig. "The most dramatic part was loading him into the crate. Pigs scream when their feet leave the ground," says Bennett, "but once he was in the crate he was fine."

HONORABLE DISCHARGE

Harrisburg, PA

San Antonio, TX

NAMES: *Fritz and Derrick*
BREED: *German shepherds*
AGE: *Mature*

TOTAL MILEAGE:
1,432

ROUTE:
San Antonio, Texas–Harrisburg, Pennsylvania

For Fritz and Derrick, long active-duty careers had come to an end. The two German shepherds, both military working dogs stationed at Lackland Air Force Base in Texas, were retiring. Both suffered poor health—Derrick was battling an aggressive form of cancer, while Fritz struggled with a degenerative neurological disorder.

Neither Derrick nor Fritz could be cured of their conditions, but through the efforts of the Austin German Shepherd Dog Rescue and several compassionate individuals, their final months would find them surrounded by love and honored for their service to our nation.

Todd Johnson is a volunteer with AGSDR and a pilot who has flown several missions for Pilots N Paws. When he heard that both dogs had been offered adoptive homes in Pennsylvania, he was determined to get them there. Knowing he couldn't make the cross-country trek alone, he posted a transport request to the PNP Web site. He planned to fly the first leg to Dallas and hoped other pilots would sign on to complete the transport.

The first response to his post left Johnson flabbergasted. Margo Walker, a businesswoman based in New York City, responded with an offer to send a Hawker 800 business jet to San Antonio to pick up the dogs and take them anywhere they needed to go. Five days later, the plane arrived in San Antonio with two pilots and an in-flight caretaker for the warrior dogs.

In just a few hours, the jet covered the 1,500-mile route that would have normally required several transfers and

Bottom: On the ground in San Antonio, Texas, Kim AmRhein, Gina Helm, and PNP pilot Todd Johnson prepare to load Fritz for the flight to Pennsylvania. AmRhein is the San Antonio coordinator for Austin German Shepherd Rescue. Two San Antonio Airport Police K9 officers also stopped by to pay their respects to the retired military service dogs.

at least a full day of flying. In Harrisburg, Pennsylvania, Derrick and Fritz were greeted by their new families, their working days through and their every need attended to.

Within a few months of arriving at their new homes, both Derrick and Fritz succumbed to their ailments, but they did receive a final tribute to their service before passing away. On November 11, 2010, Fritz and Derrick were honored on the floor of the Pennsylvania legislature. It was, after all, Veterans Day.

After serving more than a decade each in the U.S. military, Fritz (left and upper right with owner Jennifer Cox) and Derrick (lower right) lived out their lives as civilians in Pennsylvania.

"He was such a great dog, and my heart still breaks because we had such a short time with him. But I would do it all over again even knowing that we'd only have three months with him."

—*Jennifer Cox, Fritz's adoptive owner*

ERNIE'S JOURNEY

NAME: *Ernie*
BREED: *Dachshund*
AGE: *Seven years*

TOTAL MILEAGE:
316

ROUTE:
*Jacksonville, North Carolina–Wilmington, North Carolina**
*Wilmington, North Carolina–Loris, South Carolina**
Loris, South Carolina–Savannah, Georgia

Ernie was down and very nearly out. As a senior dog, surrendered to a high-kill county animal-control shelter in North Carolina, his prospects did not look rosy. It didn't help that shelter personnel labeled Ernie as aggressive. He was scheduled for euthanasia.

But Tiffeny Yohman, a Jacksonville, North Carolina, animal rescuer and former shelter employee, suspected Ernie might have got a bum rap. "Dachshunds are notorious for being fear-aggressive," explains Yohman. "In a shelter environment, they are terrified times ten."

* Ground (car) transport leg

Yohman had learned of Ernie through friends at the shelter. Aware of her passion and extensive network of contacts in the rescue community, the director and staff often call Yohman when they have a dog that's run out of options.

Yohman went immediately to work, sending e-mail blasts relating Ernie's plight to her rescue contacts. Three hundred miles away in Savannah, Georgia, she made the connection that would turn the tide for Ernie. Terry Wolf of Southern Comfort Animal Rescue was willing to take Ernie and committed to finding him a new home.

With a destination set, Operation Ernie's Journey went into action. It would take a diverse group of rescuers, fosters, and transporters to move Ernie down the southeast Atlantic coast—a group assembled by Wolf and rescue coordinator Charity Merrill. "Most rescue individuals are on chat lines or Yahoo! Groups, and we crosspost the devil out of dogs in need of rescue," says Merrill. Among her many posts was one to the Pilots N Paws board, requesting transport to Georgia.

Within twenty-four hours, Wolf and Merrill had all the transport links in place. "Terry made a miracle happen overnight," says Yohman of Wolf's transport coordination. On June 19, 2010, just one day after first speaking to Terry Wolf, Yohman went to the Onslow County Animal Control facility to spring Ernie. When the shelter attendant brought him out, he literally jumped into her arms. "He was a total love bug," she says. "He was so appreciative—almost like he knew he was getting out." Once in Yohman's car, Ernie settled into the passenger seat across from her and they headed south.

Ernie's next stop was Wilmington, North Carolina, where Yohman met up with another volunteer driver, Donna Bloomer. Bloomer had laid out a blanket for Ernie in the backseat, but in a "calm but determined" way, he climbed across the armrest and, once again, curled up in the shotgun seat.

"Senior dogs always seem to have a lot of personality, and with Ernie this was especially so," Bloomer recalls. Still, "it was impossible not to love the little guy," she says. Once situated to Ernie's liking—side by side—they made their way farther down the highway to meet Tom and Linda Scott, a couple who would foster Ernie overnight at their home in Loris, South Carolina.

Ernie may have begun the day in what, for him, were hellish conditions, but walking into the Scotts' house, he must have thought he'd died and gone to wiener dog heaven. Amiable Ernie fell right in with the Scott's *six* resident doxies. He impressed dogs and humans alike at the Scott's self-proclaimed "Wienerville Resort and Spa."

"He was pleasant, congenial, and just an ideal little soul," reports Tom. "Had arrangements not already been made for Ernie, we would have been thrilled to add him to our herd."

For sheer excitement, it's difficult to follow up a night in the company of a half a dozen wiener dogs, but the next day pilot Brett Grooms kept the thrills coming. Ernie was going to get his wings. The Scotts drove Ernie to Twin City Airport in Loris, where Ernie met PNP volunteer Grooms, who had flown from Charleston, South Carolina, to pick him up.

Ernie remained unflappable as he settled into Grooms' Cessna 172 for his first known flight. "He was a perfect passenger," reports Grooms. "He never made a sound the entire flight. Upon arrival in Savannah, he stretched his little legs and wiggled his tail—he seemed to know he was beginning a new future with a loving family."

Though they'd had little more than two hours together, Ernie had worked his magic on another of his liberators. "I tend to be a big dog type of guy," says Grooms, "and never thought a little brown, stubby legged, long-bodied dog could capture my heart like Ernie, but this awkward-shaped wiener dog did just that. Those who don't believe an animal can speak directly to your heart have never met a dog like Ernie," Grooms continues. "There was something special about him."

On the ground at Savannah/Hilton Head International Airport, Terry Wolf's daughter, Shannon, met Grooms and welcomed Ernie to Georgia. The plan was for Shannon to overnight Ernie and then drive the last leg of his transport from Savannah to her mother's Southern Comfort Animal Rescue in Glenwood, Georgia.

Ernie enjoyed a night to remember at Tom and Linda Scott's "Wienerville Resort and Spa" in Loris, South Carolina.

To pilot Grooms and everyone else who had met Ernie along the way, however, it came as no surprise that the little brown dachshund didn't quite make it to his planned destination. Both Shannon Wolf and her son Mason fell hard for Ernie. His journey would end in Savannah. They decided he was home.

Terry Wolf, in her new role as Ernie's grandmother, posted the news via e-mail to Ernie's fans up and down the Atlantic seaboard, closing out this unlikely rescue appropriately: "So cheers to Ernie—the little polite, loveable dachshund who motivated so many people and captured hearts all along the way!"

Score one for the little guy.

Top: PNP pilot Brett Grooms (left) took the handoff from Linda and Tom Scott in South Carolina, and ferried Ernie to Savannah, Georgia. Bottom left: Ernie never made it to Terry Wolf's (pictured) Southern Comfort Animal Rescue in Glenwood, Georgia. Her daughter, Shannon, decided to keep Ernie after fostering him for one night along the way. Bottom right: The amazing Ernie exhibits his skills.

"People ask, 'Why would you spend $500 of your hard-earned money to fly a single dog?' My answer: 'It means a lot to that particular dog, and it's not just about the animals—it's about all the people who are also affected by his or her transport.'

"I believe the wonderful people on the ground who spend countless hours helping to coordinate rescues are why so many pilots readily offer their aircraft, time, and money to transport animals across the United States. The ground rescuers have such passion to help animals, and that passion is infectious. Pilots also have an incredible passion to fly, and when we combine flying and animals, it makes for a wonderful blend."

—Brett Grooms, PNP pilot and Ernie liberator

CHANCE
ENCOUNTER

Indianapolis, IN

Nicholas County, KY

NAME: *Chance*
BREED: *Great Pyrenees mix*
AGE: *Puppy*

TOTAL MILEAGE:
153

ROUTE:
Nicholas County, Kentucky–Indianapolis, Indiana

The Nicholas County, Kentucky, animal shelter wouldn't normally be considered a lucky place for a dog to end up, but for a three-month-old ball of white fur appropriately named Chance, it was just the right place—at precisely the right time. Chance had entered the shelter as a stray, and when no one claimed him after the mandatory hold period, shelter volunteer Kathy Chase began trying to place the Great Pyrenees mix with a rescue group.

"The next morning, I got a rather rushed e-mail asking if I could be at the regional airport in the next county in an hour with Chance," recalls Chase. In a coincidence of timing, Pilots N Paws volunteer Bob Born was soon due to take off with an adult Pyrenees from a neighboring shelter, bound for the same Indy Great Pyrenees Rescue.

"I grabbed the puppy and raced to the airport," says Kathy, "arriving just in time to watch 'Pilot Bob' (she wouldn't learn his last name until later) land his small plane and taxi over to us. He emerged smiling, and said, 'Great day to fly!' Chance and the adult Pyrenees hopped in the rear seats, taxied away, and off they went into the wild blue yonder." Not surprisingly, Chance was adopted out shortly after arriving.

PNP pilot Bob Born (in white shirt, above) enjoyed the companionship of Chance and an adult Great Pyrenees on the rescue flight from Kentucky to Indianapolis. Rescue volunteers Kathy Chase (top left) and Barbar Eblen (top right) transported the dogs to the airport.

DORIE'S STORY

NAME: *Dorie*
BREED: *Belgian sheepdog*
AGE: *Three*

TOTAL MILEAGE:
2,006

ROUTE:

Harrisburg, Pennsylvania–Breezewood, Pennsylvania*
Breezewood, Pennsylvania–Washington, Pennsylvania*
Washington, Pennsylvania–St. Clairsville, Ohio*
St. Clairsville, Ohio–Columbus, Ohio*
Columbus, Ohio–Kansas City, Missouri
Kansas City, Missouri–Lawrence, Kansas*
Lawrence, Kansas–Guymon, Oklahoma
Guymon, Oklahoma–Santa Fe, New Mexico
Santa Fe, New Mexico–Albuquerque, New Mexico*
Albuquerque, New Mexico–Tucson, Arizona

There are a million reasons why pets wind up homeless. For Dorie, a rangy, coal-black Belgian sheepdog, one reason was simply the intensity of her staring eyes.

* Ground (car) transport leg

98

Until early 2009 Dorie led a vagabond life, passed from one home to another by owners who had initially been attracted by her intelligence, attentiveness, and energy, but ultimately frustrated that the dog didn't turn out to be what they had expected.

Dorie spent the first three years of her life in a chaotic home so overpopulated with pets that local authorities finally forced the owner to remove several dogs. Adopted by a family in South Carolina, she seemed to have improved her lot in life. But the adoption didn't take. Her new owners became so disconcerted by the way the large herding dog stared at their toddler that they decided to give her up.

Next was a short stay in Connecticut. Owner allergies necessitated another move after only a few weeks. A family in New York answered a newspaper ad about Dorie and she was packed up again. After two weeks, that family decided Dorie's energy level was more than they could handle.

Dorie's overattentive gaze was partially responsible for one of her many busted adoptions.

As its name suggests, the Belgian sheepdog is a herding dog. As a breed, they are considered intelligent and highly trainable. They are known for their alertness and for their penchant to seek out and maintain eye contact with their owners. For these reasons and others, they are often used as assistance dogs or in police and search-and-rescue work.

But despite her pedigree and potential, after being cast out of four homes in the span of a few months, Dorie seemed to be running out of chances.

In the course of moving from home to home, Dorie's history had become muddled. By this time, in addition to being misunderstood by owners unfamiliar with her breed, she had also been without the anti-epileptic and hypothyroid medications that had been prescribed years earlier. Without her medication, she was having violent seizures multiple times daily.

Unable to cope with the dog and unsure what to do, Dorie's New York family asked a friend for help. She was a dog breeder in Pennsylvania, and after hearing Dorie's story, she agreed to take the dog in.

There's a point in every rescue story when the tide of misfortune is turned. According to Lynnette Bennett, head of the North American Belgian Sheepdog Rescue (NAB-SDR), that point was reached when the Good Samaritan in Pennsylvania welcomed Dorie into her home. "This woman," Bennett says, "saved Dorie's life."

The woman took Dorie to her vet who diagnosed the dog's health problems and prescribed medication to get her seizures under control. By this time, the woman had fallen hard for Dorie and wanted to keep her. But she feared for the dog's safety. She was a breeder of terriers and worried that if Dorie had a seizure when she wasn't home, the dogs might mistake her for prey and attack. She tracked down Dorie's breeder for advice. She was shocked at his response. He insisted that the dog be put down and pressured her to keep Dorie's health problems to herself. That's when Dorie's benefactor had the good fortune to come across a force of nature named Lynnette Bennett.

As head of the NABSDR, Lynnette Bennett has rescued, fostered, rehabilitated, and trained hundreds of dogs—most of them Belgians. She's passionate about the breed, and few people know it better. Bennett works full-time to care for and train the dogs, and maintains a nationwide network of other volunteers, foster homes, and Belgian advocates. She does all of this on a volunteer basis. And she does it all from a wheelchair.

The woman in Pennsylvania recounted Dorie's history to Bennett over the phone. More than two thousand miles away, in Tucson, Arizona, Bennett listened with an open heart and mind. And while she was aggrieved at the transient life the dog had led, she wasn't particularly surprised to hear that Dorie had been given up so many times.

"Every one of this dog's owners had fallen in love with it," explains Bennett. "But Belgian sheepdogs are herding dogs. They have some very specific traits that don't work for all families."

When Dorie's caretaker told her about the big dog's propensity to stare, she smiled knowingly. "Herding dogs love to maintain eye contact," she says. "They will always seek out your gaze and that does unnerve some people."

With that call to Bennett, Dorie was on her way to a new life—and, as it turns out, a higher purpose. In addition to running NABSDR, Lynnette Bennett trains Belgian sheepdogs to be service dogs. As she pieced together Dorie's checkered history, she became more convinced that the dog was a prime prospect to be a companion animal.

Bennett began to work out a transport scenario to move Dorie from Pennsylvania to her home in Tucson. She found volunteer drivers to get the dog as far as Columbus, Ohio. She had also posted transport requests on the Pilots N Paws message board. From his home in Kansas City, Missouri, pilot Sam Taylor saw the request. As it turned out, he was going to be flying two English cocker spaniels from Kansas City to Columbus in just a few days. Working together, Taylor, Bennett, and the woman coordinating the cocker spaniel transport settled on a schedule.

On the afternoon of March 26, 2009, Sam Taylor loaded Dorie into the backseat of his 1964 Piper Cherokee and took off from the Columbus airport bound for Kansas City. It was the second leg of Sam's first mission for Pilots N Paws. He immediately developed an affinity for his passenger. "She was a beautiful dog," Sam remembers. "Pretty mellow but also very aware of everything that was going on. It's like she knew she was being rescued."

By the time he had landed safely back in Kansas City, he was downright smitten. It was nearly 9 P.M. when they arrived, so he and Bennett had already decided that Dorie would stay the night with the Taylors before continuing on her journey.

Less population density and greater distance between cities makes finding volunteer pilots more difficult west of the Mississippi. To make matters worse, several wildfires in Texas in the spring of 2009 were making flying toward the Southwest tricky. Bennett e-mailed Taylor to say that she was looking for a foster home for Dorie in Kansas City until conditions improved. Sam e-mailed back immediately. Dorie would be welcome in his home as long as necessary.

It took three weeks for Bennett to work out a transport plan to get

Top: Wanda and Sam Taylor fell in love with Dorie during a three-week fostering stint in Kansas City. Bottom: PNP pilot J. P. Held flew Dorie from Guyman, Oklahoma, to Santa Fe, New Mexico.

101

Dorie the rest of the way to Tucson. By that time, Dorie had come to feel like part of the Taylor family, enjoying the company of their two golden retrievers and accompanying Sam on his morning runs. "By the time transportation had been worked out, my wife and I had both fallen in love with her," remembers Taylor with a laugh. "We were ready to call Lynnette and tell her that Dorie had run away."

Instead, the Taylors handed Dorie off to a NABSDR foster volunteer in nearby Lawrence, Kansas. A week later, Dorie was in the air again, first flying from Lawrence to Guymon, Oklahoma, and then, with another volunteer pilot, on to Santa Fe, New Mexico.

That pilot drove Dorie to Albuquerque and delivered her to a foster volunteer—a retired air force pilot disabled in Vietnam who lives up in the mountains and runs a de facto shelter, taking in "dogs that nobody wants." After a few days spent among this small pack of castoffs, Dorie was driven back to Albuquerque, where she was put on a flight to Tucson. It had taken twenty drivers, pilots, and foster volunteers and nearly forty days and nights to get Dorie from Pennsylvania to Tucson. Lynnette Bennett—the woman who cobbled together this unlikely journey, was there to greet her at the airport.

During the course of Dorie's odyssey, Bennett had stayed in constant contact with the dog's caretakers. According to Bennett, the big black dog left a trail of broken hearts all along the way. "Sam [Taylor] is not the only one who fell in love with her instantly," says Bennett. "Despite all her handicaps, she's a dream dog, and every driver, pilot, or foster household she met between Pennsylvania and here fell for her."

Bennett began Dorie's training immediately and found her a quick study. "Dorie stayed here for a few weeks, learning to pick up a cell phone and hand it to someone, open and close doors, ignore food dropped on the floor, walk very close to a wheelchair, turn light switches on and off, brace herself to steady her owner for transfers from wheelchair to toilet or bed, and to take half steps one at a time, halting after each one. She was an extremely bright dog and eager to learn."

"Successful rescue takes an entire team. In my cases I may be the one who puts the pieces together, but without all the caring volunteers evaluating, teaching basic obedience commands, driving, fostering (especially longer than planned), going to the vet, getting to airports, flying, and so on . . . well, there'd be no pieces to put together."

—*Lynnette Bennett,*
North American Belgian Sheepdog Rescue

"In all those homes, I don't think she'd ever had all her needs met before," Bennett says. "It's not that people didn't care or didn't love her, but this is a highly specialized breed. These dogs aren't content to be pets—they want to work."

Bennett places her "graduate" dogs in homes all across the country, but for the well-traveled Dorie, she was able to find a perfect match right there in Tucson. "This woman had lost her twelve-year-old service dog and says that Dorie got her through that loss by loving her, as well as providing help with fragile mobility," Bennett reports. "Dorie also goes out and returns with the paper and mail by herself and has an extensive fan club on her owner's regular city bus rides."

As for Bennett, she's delighted to have Dorie living in the same city where she can visit every few months. "Dorie's life is so settled now," she says, "that she was able to get off her medication and has remained seizure-free."

It's nice to be loved, but for some dogs it's even more important to be needed. After so many years adrift and misunderstood, Dorie is finally both.

THE
ROUND-TRIPPER

NAME: *Sammie*
BREED: *Dachshund*
AGE: *Two*

TOTAL MILEAGE:
834

ROUTE:
Auburn, California–Vacaville, California*
Vacaville, California–Fullerton, California
Fullerton, California–Vacaville, California

ammy Rieser has an eye for dachshunds. As a volunteer adviser for Southern
California Dachshund Relief, she often consults with shelters that have taken in
dachshunds, a breed notoriously uncomfortable—and sometimes ill-tempered—in
shelter conditions. So in the fall of 2009, when she saw a craigslist posting from the
Placer County, California, animal shelter seeking foster care for a formerly abused two-
year-old dachshund, she inquired about his situation.

* Ground (car) transport leg

Sammie's life had gotten off to a rough start. He'd entered the shelter as a cruelty seizure, having been abused and neglected. The neglect had led to severe health problems—an untreated bite in the hind quarters from another dog had resulted in a massive infection. His tail had to be amputated, and reconstructive surgery was required on his rear end. As bad as that sounds, he was lucky. "Typically, shelter resources and expertise would not allow such major surgery," says Rieser. "If the dog couldn't be placed with a rescue, he would be PTS [put to sleep]."

But the shelter staff wasn't about to let that happen. "They rallied around Sammie, and the vets there did the surgery gratis," says Rieser. "They loved him at the shelter; and even though they knew his medical history would make placing him in an adoptive home difficult, they were determined to try."

When Rieser saw Sammie on craigslist, she pressed Southern California Dachshund Relief to take him into their program. "Initially, they resisted as they were under the impression he was incontinent," she says, "but after further review and investigation with the shelter staff, it turned out that was not the case."

Rieser offered to foster Sammie and drove three hours north to Auburn, California, to pick him up. Her instincts about Sammie turned out to be well-founded. "He had such a wonderful temperament and outgoing personality," she says. "The nickname that the shelter staff had given him, 'Wigglebutt,' was totally appropriate. He greeted me wiggling so hard his little body was an 'S' curve."

Before finally landing in his forever home, Sammie would log some frequent-flier miles over central California.

Once home with Rieser, Sammie quickly became one of the family, fitting in beautifully with her other dogs and cats. "He was such a joy to be around," she says.

Unfortunately for Rieser, their time with Sammie would turn out to be brief. Every foster volunteer knows that letting go is an inevitable part of the job. As it turns out, SCDR director Dena Delgado had found a home for Sammie about the same time Rieser was picking him up in Auburn. Delgado had also arranged for a Pilots N Paws pilot to fly Sammie to a rescue volunteer in Southern California. He would spend a week or so there, then be moved on to his forever home.

"I was extremely sad to part with him," Rieser recalls. "A week later, I took him to the Vacaville Airport, where we hooked up with Ed McDermott, his pilot, and off he went to Los Angeles."

McDermott remembers that meeting and the pain of the parting. "It was obvious she had become attached to Sammie," the pilot says. "She even had him dressed up with a red bandanna for his journey. She expressed her reluctance to let Sammie go, but she

Top: PNP pilot Ed McDermott rounds up passengers. Bottom: Tammy Rieser snuggles Sammie and a fellow traveler.

knew she had to. So I told her if the adoption didn't work out, I'd fly him back."

Sammie was gone, but far from forgotten. Rieser compulsively checks SCDR's Web site to keep tabs on dogs in the rescue's care. She felt a pang of heartache whenever she clicked on Sammie and saw his status as "Adoption Pending," an indication that he was serving out a trial period of two weeks with his new home before adoption became official.

"Then one day when I checked on Sammie's adoption status, it said, 'Available for Adoption' again!" Rieser says excitedly. "I immediately called Dena [Delgado] to inquire, and she advised that, for whatever reason, the adopters changed their mind. I told her if that was the case I wanted to adopt Sammie. I then e-mailed Ed McDermott with Pilots N Paws and asked if, on his next transport, he would fly Sammie back up to me."

McDermott was as good as his word, and on December 5, 2009, little Sammie, the tailless doxie with the wiggly bottom, came winging his way back to where he once belonged—and always will belong—with Tammy Rieser.

Today, Sammie and Tammy are near constant companions, and the little dachshund wiggles his way into the heart of everyone he meets. He even participates in the local Humane Society's Paws to Read children's reading program, snuggling up with primary school kids for story time as they work to improve their reading skills. "He is the first-ever dachshund to be admitted to the program," points out his mother with unconcealed pride.

Who says you need a tail to have a happy ending?

Tammy and Sammie share some story time with third-grader Emma Camacho as part of a Paws to Read children's reading program.

OUT OF
NEW ORLEANS

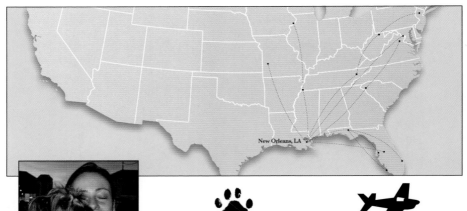

NAME: *Various*
BREED: *Many*
AGE: *All*

TOTAL MILEAGE:
10,000+

ROUTES:
New Orleans, Louisiana–Knoxville, Tennessee–Morganton, West Virginia–Caldwell, New Jersey
New Orleans–Memphis, Tennessee–Davenport, Iowa
New Orleans–Clemson, South Carolina–Warrenton, Virginia
New Orleans–Nevada, Missouri
New Orleans–Marianna, Florida
Marianna, Florida–Tampa, Naples, and West Palm Beach, Florida
New Orleans–Lakeland, Florida

B y the time the rising sun shimmered on the waters of Lake Pontchartrain, at least one plane had already lifted off, bound for Tennessee. Back on the ground, a squadron of pilots moved quietly among the nearly two dozen small aircraft, conducting preflight inspections. This wasn't a military operation, but with the urgency and sense of mission in the air it might have been.

171 dogs caught one-way flights out of New Orleans on September 18, 2010. Among those assisting on the ground were (top from left) Julliana Galli, Linda Barbaro, and Rhonda Goodland. Top right: Chris Goodland gets a good-bye kiss. Center right: PNP cofounder Jon Wehrenberg loads pups bound for Iowa.

Pilots weren't the only ones up early on September 18, 2010, the day of PNP's Gulf Coast Rescue Flyway. By dawn, trucks and vans filled with dogs from the region's overcrowded animal shelters dotted the edge of a dedicated ramp of New Orleans's former municipal airport. A battalion of volunteers moved along the thin strip of grass bordering the airfield—each with at least one dog at the end of a leash. Petting, hugging, holding, whispering words of encouragement . . . these troops, too, were critical to the mission. By 8 A.M., dogs, people, smiles, tears, and cameras were everywhere.

Debi Boies, cofounder of PNP, played field marshal that day, matching planes with pups and signaling pilots when it was their time to take to the sky. Rescue volunteers representing twelve different shelters sought the tail number of "their" pilot's plane, delivered each dog's dossier to the airmen and women, and helped load passengers. With each takeoff, the ground crew and remaining pilots erupted in a spontaneous cheer as the departing pilot dipped a wing and rose steadily through the crystalline blue sky. With each plane, another batch of lives was reclaimed.

Hundreds of miles away, volunteers with fifteen different animal-rescue organizations in six states and the District of Columbia anxiously awaited the exiles from New Orleans. Brighter futures, better lives, and the promise of forever homes lay ahead.

For many of the dogs, this would be only the first flight of the day. Transfers were made with other pilots in other states. In all, fifty-four planes would take part in moving dogs across the country in this one-day intensive animal-saving mission.

"It was a perfect day," says Boies. "We will most assuredly remember the incredible sight as the sun rose that Saturday morning in September."

Lucky dogs await loading in a climate-controlled kennel trailer.

Departing dogs said good-bye with kisses and waves. Above: Volunteer puppy wrangler Nathaniel Rodrigue from Ponchatoula, Louisiana. Bottom right: Dawn in New Orleans on departure day.

Participating Animal Rescues and Shelters

Plaquemines Animal Welfare Society (PAWS), Belle Chasse, Louisiana
Jefferson Parish Shelter East, Elmwood, Louisiana
Jefferson Parish Shelter West, Marrero, Louisiana
Don't Be Cruel Sanctuary, Albany, Louisiana
Tangipahoa Parish Animal Control Shelter, Hammond, Louisiana
East Baton Rouge Parish Animal Control Shelter, Baton Rouge, Louisiana
Northside Humane Society, Baton Rouge, Louisiana
Lafayette Animal Control Shelter, Lafayette, Louisiana
Rescued Dogs Adoption Center, Mandeville, Louisiana
Kaplan Animal Control Shelter, Kaplan, Louisiana
St. Bernard Parish Animal Control Shelter, Violet, Louisiana
St. Tammany Parish Department of Animal Services Shelter, Abita Springs, Louisiana

Receiving Groups and Rescues

Lucky Dog Animal Rescue, Washington, D.C.
PetConnect Rescue, Potomac, Maryland
Homeless Animal Rescue Team, Washington, D.C.
Lakeland SPCA, Lakeland, Florida
Humane Society of Tampa Bay, Tampa, Florida
Humane Society of Pinellas County, Clearwater, Florida
Suncoast Animal League, Palm Harbor, Florida
SPCA Tampa Bay, Largo, Florida
Humane Society of Naples, Naples, Florida
A Second Chance for Puppies and Kittens Rescue, West Palm Beach, Florida
PetResQ, Inc., Tenafly, New Jersey
Friends of Homeless Animals, Princeton, New Jersey
King's Harvest Ministries, Davenport, Iowa
Lab and All Breed Rescue Network, Brighton, Tennessee
Second Chance Barnyard, El Dorado Springs, Missouri

Special thanks to

Subaru: Ground transportation in New Orleans, hotels for pilot volunteers, and catered breakfast.
Petmate: Donation of all crates used during transports.
AeroPremier Jet Center: Ramp services, fuel discounts, and welcome barbecue.

Top left: PNP cofounder Debi Boies (left) and volunteer transport coordinator Terrie Varnado pause for a quick snap during a hectic day. Bottom: Chipmunk, the last dog to be loaded, says good-bye.

SAVING CHRISTMAS

NAME: *Christmas/Killian*
BREED: *Doberman*
AGE: *Puppy*

TOTAL MILEAGE:
307

ROUTE:
Elizabethton, Tennessee–Pittsburgh, Pennsylvania

Hard-luck cases are something of a specialty for Donna Lohmann. Dobermans are, too. Over the years, Lohmann has fostered ten Dobermans, and along the way dealt with just about every ailment or injustice that can befall a dog. "Every one of them came in in terrible condition," she says. "When they leave for a new home they're just so healthy and happy. It touches your heart."

But it can break your heart, too. Lohmann is still haunted by one story that didn't have a happy ending. "I took in a dog who was starved and mangy—he was a real wreck," she remembers. "I nursed him back to health and he got adopted to a good family . . . and then ten months later he passed away from cancer."

After that experience, Lohmann took a break from fostering for a while, content to spend time with her two resident Dobies—a male and a female, both rescues. But she still had a weakness for hard-luck stories. One day in early 2010, she was looking at the Web site of Distinguished Doberman Rescue, located not far from her home in western Pennsylvania, when she saw a dog and couldn't look away. "I saw this sweet face, and it reminded me of the one I'd lost," she says. "Then I read his story and thought, 'I have to help him.'" Not only that, she thought, "I have to have him."

The story went like this: On a snowy night about a week before Christmas 2009, the young (seven to nine months old) dog was abandoned outside the Elizabethton, Tennessee, Animal Shelter. He was wrapped in a blanket, starving, and unable to walk. Later that night, someone driving by saw something move on the blanket and stopped to investigate. The shelter was closed for the night, but the Good Samaritan took the dog home and returned him to the shelter the next morning.

Seeing that the dog was of the Doberman breed, the shelter contacted the Doberman Assistance Network to ask if the rescue could take the dog into their system. DAN responded, working with a local rescue in Tennessee to pull the dog from the shelter and paying for a veterinary exam. The dog was severely malnourished, and he suffered from a bad case of mange, which had caused skin infections. The pads of his paws were so infected, in fact, that he was unable to walk. But it could have been much worse. His spirits were good, and with proper care the vet expected a full recovery. DAN held an online fundraiser to help name the dog. Members suggested a name and pledged an amount toward that name. When the twenty-four-hour contest had ended, the dog's new name was "Christmas."

When DAN member Sue Szyklinski, who also runs the Distinguished Doberman Rescue, a private rescue near Pittsburgh, Pennsylvania, put out a call for a foster volunteer, Nancy Robson offered to take Christmas in. With a foster home lined up, Szyklinski posted a transport request to the PNP forum to get Christmas from Tennessee to Pennsylvania.

Pittsburgh-based pilots Keith and Vicki McPherson saw the request on the PNP forum and signed on to fly the entire transport. With the weather unseasonably cooperative and both Keith and Vicki on Christmas vacation, they scheduled the flight immediately. Two days

A week before Christmas, a malnourished Doberman was abandoned in the middle of the night outside the Elizabethton (Tennessee) Animal Shelter.

after Christmas 2009, "Christmas" the Doberman arrived in Pennsylvania aboard the McPherson's Piper Seneca II.

Nancy Robson met them on the ground at Allegheny County Airport just outside Pittsburgh. Over the ensuing weeks, Christmas thrived under Robson's care, gaining muscle mass and moving steadily toward a full recovery. It wasn't long before Robson and Szyklinski decided that Christmas was well enough to be made available for adoption.

That's when Donna Lohmann entered the story. Szyklinski was delighted to hear from the veteran Doberman foster mom. "She's a wonderful adopter," Szyklinski says. "She treats her Doberkids just like they are her human children."

Lohmann decided to give her new "Doberkid" a new name shortly after adopting him. "He's small for a Doberman—I think he was the runt of the litter—but he's a feisty little thing, so we came up with 'Killian,' which means 'small but fierce.'"

Killian's first year in his new home was a prolonged exercise in learning to trust again, says Lohmann. "He's doing much better, but he is still afraid of some things—still a little skittish." The cold December night he was abandoned may also still linger in his subconscious. "He absolutely does not like to be outside when it's cold," she says.

Top: The dog christened "Christmas" on December 27, 2009, the day of her rescue flight to Pennsylvania. Bottom: According to his new owner, Christmas still doesn't like snow and cold.

Killian has found a mentor in Lohmann's other male Doberman.

"They love each other," she says. "Killian follows him around the house and does everything he does. They're always together."

As for Killian's Dobie sister, "She's adjusting," says Lohmann. "She's figuring out that, unlike other dogs I've fostered, he's not leaving."

Killian, the dog formerly known as "Christmas," enjoys the summer sun and her two adopted Dobie siblings.

LEARNING TO FLY

NAME: *Ed/Kite*
BREED: *German shepherd*
AGE: *1 year*

TOTAL MILEAGE:
640

ROUTE:
Cozad, Nebraska–Longmont, Colorado
Longmont, Colorado–Kanab, Utah

The one-year-old German shepherd on the examining table had been hobbled by a mysterious malady. All anyone knew for sure was that he was "down in the back"— his hind legs had suddenly stopped working. As the veterinarian and the dog's owner discussed his condition and his fate, the owner, a Nebraska farmer on a tight budget, made the painful decision to euthanize if the dog wasn't back up after the weekend.

A veterinary technician in the small-town animal clinic, Betsy Quandt, had stood by the examining table and listened to the exchange. She maintained professional composure. It wasn't the first time she'd heard an animal's life discussed in the exam room. But while she understood the position of the owner and the vet, she couldn't shake the belief that this dog had more to give. When the weekend passed and the dog hadn't improved, she asked the vet if she could have a week to try to find another option. He conferred with the owner, and they agreed. "Ed" had one week.

"I'd recently experienced how full a handicapped animal's life can be with an injured stray cat that I'd taken home from work several months before," says Quandt. "I was unable to take Ed in, however, because I was allowed only one dog in my current living situation." Instead, Quandt posted Ed's story on handicappedpets.com, a forum she'd discovered while seeking resources for her cat.

"I called all my animal-loving friends, called or sent e-mails to every rescue I could find in Nebraska, then to any that looked promising anywhere!" says Quandt, who lives in Kearney, about twenty minutes from the clinic where she works in Overton, Nebraska. "Ed was a tough case whose needs and outcome were unsure, so my answers were mostly no or silence."

Ed's week was almost up when Quandt received an e-mail from Laura Bradshaw of Healing HEART Sanctuary in Kanab, Utah. She asked Quandt to call her the following day to discuss Ed's situation.

For so many stray and unwanted animals, the difference between life and death hinges on the compassionate intervention of one person. For Ed, Betsy Quandt was that person. She had given him a second chance. Laura Bradshaw would be the next person in a long line who would parlay that second chance into a reclaimed life.

Bradshaw told Quandt that, although she wasn't able to accommodate Ed at the sanctuary, she was confident that she could find him a foster home in Kanab. That way, she reasoned, the volunteers at Healing HEART could still assist in his rehabilitation. In short order, Bradshaw had found a foster volunteer, a friend who offered to house the dog as a personal favor.

Healing HEART Sanctuary is an extraordinary facility devoted to getting both animals and children back on their feet. The sanctuary takes in and rehabilitates rescued animals that have been injured or disabled. Some are adopted out to appropriate homes, and others stay on as part of the sanctuary's on-site program. During an animal's rehabilitative time at Healing HEART, children who are physically, mentally, or emotionally challenged get the chance to interact with, care for, and help in the recovery process of the animals.

It's nearly a thousand highway miles from Kearney, Nebraska, to Kanab, Utah, and no one liked the prospect of driving Ed. A member of the handicappedpets.com message board, where Ed's plight was posted, suggested they turn to Pilots N Paws for transport, and in short order three PNP pilots offered to help. A legion of other volunteers offered assistance with overnight fostering, transportation to and from airports, and even backup ground transportation if the weather was too rough to cross the Rocky Mountains.

"I was amazed at how many people stepped up," says Bradshaw. "We had a Plan B, C, and D."

But Ed wasn't out of the woods yet. On the very cold February morning that he was originally scheduled to fly Ed out of Nebraska, pilot Mike Gannon was signaled on the ramp that fire had broken out in his 1969 Cessna's exhaust system and was trailing out of his tailpipe. No one was hurt, but the flight was scrubbed and Gannon's plane was temporarily grounded.

A few frantic phone calls later, Plan B fell into place. Joe Marley, a PNP pilot who had signed up to foster Ed overnight at his home in Longmont, Colorado, agreed to fly all the way to Nebraska to pick the dog up. Leaving Longmont the next day after getting off work, Marley landed in central Nebraska about two and a half hours later.

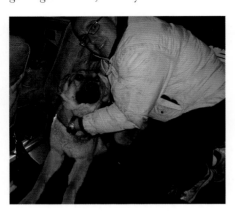

PNP pilot Joe Marley flew Ed from Cozad, Nebraska, to Longmont, Colorado.

"We had to change airports a couple of times—one had weather issues, another was closed," remembers Marley. "Betsy went out of her way to drive to a different airport in a different town after dark to deliver Ed to me—she's a gutsy girl."

At the municipal airport in Cozad, Nebraska, the two lifted Ed into the back of Marley's Cherokee Six, and at last Ed was off, heading west into the darkening night. It was nearly 9 P.M. when Marley touched down at Vance Brand Municipal Airport in Longmont.

Ed spent the next two nights at the Marley household. "My kids immediately fell in love with him," he says, "especially my two-year-old daughter, who could only call him 'Eggie.' Ed was gentle as can be. He had an incredible disposition . . . and he received nonstop attention for the few days he stayed with us."

In the span of those few days, Ed was also growing noticeably more steady on his feet. "He wasn't strong enough to run or jump," says Marley, "but he could walk without assistance. When we left to go to the airport, he was recovered enough that he walked himself into the Suburban, including a step up."

His recovery had indeed begun while in Nebraska, awaiting transport, according to Betsy Quandt. The vet and Ed's owner discussed the young shepherd's improving condition, but the farmer ultimately decided that proceeding with the rescue plans would be the best thing for the dog.

It was pilot Drew Armstrong's job to fly Ed "over the rock pile." On Friday, February 26, 2010, with a weather report for CAVU (ceiling and visibility unlimited), Armstrong and a friend took off from Grand Junction, Colorado, on the Western Slope of the Continental Divide, and flew east over the Rocky Mountains to pick up Ed in Longmont, where Marley met him at the airport.

Ed arrives in Kanab, Utah. "I keep this photo on my bulletin board," says pilot Drew Armstrong, "to remind me of a special dog given a special opportunity."

"I had brought a kennel but Ed just hopped up onto the rear seats so we just tethered him to keep him from trying to come up and help us fly the plane," recalls Armstrong. "He was a great passenger. He just curled up on the seat for the entire trip."

Flight time to Kanab was a little more than two and a half hours. Armstrong relished the time with Ed, whom he called "a very special dog." He admits that it was "sweet sorrow" to turn Ed over to the "strangers" waiting at the airport in Kanab.

As Armstrong's Bonanza touched down, the group let out a collective sigh of relief—and then a cheer. "So many people had come to the aid of this one dog, for this one mission to get him here," explains Laura Bradshaw. "There were so many times the ball could have been dropped, but someone always stepped up when things broke down. That's what was so cool about it."

Ed's welcoming party included Laura Bradshaw and a handful of friends and Healing HEART volunteers. Kanab resident Linda Gail Stevens was among them. At Bradshaw's urging, she'd come to greet Ed's plane and take some pictures, bringing along her large six-year-old shepherd mix, Kobe.

"We saw the plane come down and got our first glimpse of Ed," Stevens recalls. "He was looking through the window as they taxied up to us. The pilot got out and they very carefully lifted him out and put him down on the tarmac. He was on his legs, walking, a little wobbly but better than we had anticipated." As soon as Ed was on the ground, Kobe ran over and the two big dogs went nose-to-nose. "They greeted each other as if they were long-lost friends," says Stevens. "They were instantly bonded. I've never seen anything like it."

Laura Bradshaw remembers the fateful moment when Ed met Kobe . . . and Stevens met Ed. "She looked at me and said, 'So this dog *has* a foster home?'"

Ed gets a warm welcome from Laura Bradshaw, director of Healing HEART Sanctuary in Kanab, Utah.

Bradshaw answered that while she did have a foster home lined up for Ed, she suspected that the person who had volunteered the service might be relieved if she found another option.

Linda Gail Stevens with Ed and Kobe.

> ## "Everyone knew almost instantaneously [that Ed belonged with Linda Gail and Kobe]. . . . It was just so perfect."
>
> —*Laura Bradshaw, executive director,*
> *Healing HEART Sanctuary*

Well-laid plans have a way of changing quickly in the world of animal rescue, and on this bright afternoon in southern Utah, it became clear to all assembled that Ed's future lay with Linda Gail Stevens and Kobe. A quick round of discussions among Stevens, Bradshaw, and the intended foster volunteer led to a unanimous decision. "An hour later," recalls Stevens, "Laura was on my doorstep with Ed."

Once prematurely registered as euthanized, Ed is now the picture of health and vitality.

Looking back on that day, Linda Gail Stevens admits that she foresaw Ed's fate the moment he exited Drew Armstrong's airplane. "I can't really tell you how or why, but I knew—I knew at that point that he was going to be mine."

Ed didn't end up spending much time at Healing HEART Sanctuary. As he made his way across the Rocky Mountain west, he was also slowly but steadily getting better on his own. By the time he landed in Utah, his mobility was almost entirely restored. Two vets examined him in Utah, and though neither could say definitively what had paralyzed his back legs, the consensus was that Ed had experienced some sort of soft-tissue injury, and that when the swelling subsided, so did his paralysis. It's amazing to think that this relatively minor, temporary affliction would have—without the intervention of a big-hearted veterinary technician in Nebraska—cost this young, strong animal his life.

That's something Stevens will never forget. "Without Betsy, I wouldn't have this remarkable animal," she says. "It's thanks to her that I am now living with these two beautiful souls."

"I'm so glad that things worked out for Ed. I don't feel like a hero, though. I didn't have any of the right tools to help him. It felt like a losing battle until Laura came along. If it wasn't for her, this story would have been a heartbreaker."

—*Betsy Quandt*

During her short time caring for Ed in Nebraska, Betsy Quandt only managed to get one picture of them together.

Months later, it came as a surprise to precisely no one when Stevens officially adopted Ed—another case of the common phenomenon affectionately known as "foster failure."

"I'd tell everyone, 'I'm just fostering him,' and they'd give me a look and say, 'That dog is yours. You're not giving him up.'" Stevens herself can't quite explain her hesitation in making matters permanent. Likely, it just took her head awhile to catch up to her heart.

Top: Big Ed was a definite hit with the kids (Marissa Cox and Waylon White) when he accompanied Laura Bradshaw on a visit to a Head Start program in Kanab, Utah. Bottom: Ed romps on the banks of the Colorado River in Arizona.

Since adopting Ed, Linda Gail Stevens has joined the staff of Healing HEART Sanctuary as an animal caregiver. As for Ed, she says, "He has never shown any signs of any problems at all. He is completely recovered." Still, looking through his veterinary files once the adoption was completed, she got a chilling reminder of just how close he had come. "On his file," she says, "he was already registered as euthanized."

A new life warrants celebration, and in their own way, Linda Gail Stevens and Kobe celebrate Ed's new life every day. To go along with that new life, Stevens believes that Ed wanted a new name—a name not tied to the negative energies residual from his old life. "I wanted to give him a name that was just for him," she explains. She spent several weeks thinking up names that suited him.

She was still weighing the contenders one day as she walked with her dogs near their high-desert home. "I was watching him," she says, "and we have sort of open scrubland here, and he was running through the scrubs, and he just appeared to *flow* across the earth, hardly touching the ground. He looked like a kite before it lifts up, and suddenly he jumped over a scrub bush, and it was like a kite taking off, and he kind of flew with the wind. I spontaneously called the name, 'Kite!' and he immediately looked at me and came over, and I thought, 'OK, you like that one. That one's yours.'"

Asked if she believes in fate, Stevens waits a long moment before answering. "I don't know what you want to call it . . . but I've been told that this animal made its way to me—that whether I wanted it or not, this dog found me and that's it. So I'm happy with that."

"Having to jump through so many hoops meant that many more people became involved. This thing needed to bless more people along the way before it played out."

—*Laura Bradshaw, Healing HEART Sanctuary*

AFTERWORD

I met Sam Taylor for the first time on the last day of 2009. I'd had the idea for this book just days before while talking to Sam's wife, Wanda, who I'd come to know while working on a previous project. During a casual conversation, Wanda mentioned Sam's unusual volunteer work and my ears perked up. Flying dogs? I had to hear more.

We met for breakfast at a restaurant near the Taylors' home in Kansas City. I'd come prepared for an interview—notebook and digital recorder in hand. The audio file from that morning provides the perfect background buzz of a busy breakfast diner—coffee cups clanking, silverware clinking, the white noise of a dozen different conversations. Not ideal circumstances for an interview. But listening closely to that recording I can hear the excitement in Sam's voice as he recounted the rescue flights he'd been making for the nine months previous. He talked with obvious affection about the dogs he'd flown—the Siberian husky mother and her five-day-old pups; the hundred-pound bloodhound that untethered himself from the backseat and tried to climb on to Sam's lap during landing; the Belgian sheepdog he'd flown, fostered, fallen in love with, and desperately wanted to keep; and the Labradoodle that *did* become a permanent part of the Taylor home after being turned away from a previously arranged foster home.

It wasn't as easy to get Sam to talk about himself, but over that and subsequent meetings his story did emerge with some coaxing. He was ex-navy, ex-Pentagon, and a retired high school teacher. He'd flown navy helicopters during the Vietnam War years—as a search-and-rescue pilot—but he'd also earned his pilot's license for fixed-wing aircraft. In the years following his twenty-year military career, while working as a teacher in Pennsylvania and Ohio, he had flown whenever circumstances and budget allowed—first in a rented plane and later in a well-used two-seater he'd bought in Tennessee. But by 2008, his flight hours had dwindled—despite the fact that he had retired from teaching several years earlier. "I always had the pilot's license in my pocket, but just never used it," he says. "Even with a bird in the hangar, I had, like a lot of pilots, lost that purpose for flying. The $100 hamburger had lost its appeal." When he heard about Pilots N Paws in March 2009, he rediscovered his purpose. He logged well over three hundred flight hours before the end of that year. In the previous year, he had flown thirty-nine. The search-and-rescue pilot was back on duty.

I loved hearing Sam's stories, but I was, of course, secretly hoping for more. As our first meeting wound down, I got the invitation I wanted. He asked if I'd like to accompany him on an upcoming rescue flight. Several weeks later, we were driving from Kansas City to Leavenworth, Kansas, where Sam kept his plane. My education—about Pilots N Paws, airborne animal transport, and the esoteric world of private pilots, small planes, and small airfields—had begun.

On the drive to Leavenworth, I asked a lot of questions—about his experiences in the military, about owning and maintaining a small plane, about the physics of flight. I tried not to sound like an idiot. *What exactly was a nautical mile? And if it was nautical, why was it used in the sky?* Sam was patient and genial and made things easy to understand. He had been a high school teacher for eleven years, after all.

It was cold that morning, and the airfield manager, an animal lover who approved of Sam's volunteer work, had pulled Sam's plane inside the hangar the night before to warm the engine oil. While Sam checked flight conditions in the office, I wandered into the small hangar. There were five or six airplanes inside—gleaming, lean, efficient-looking machines. A few were undergoing some sort of maintenance—parts lay nearby, engines exposed. I was clueless but impressed. Sam found me a few minutes later, checking out a very slick-looking plane that I later learned was a Cirrus SR22. "That's not my plane," he said, and then with no small degree of pride, gestured beyond it and said, "Here she is."

November-Seven-Six-Zero-Niner-Whiskey, Sam's plane, is a Piper Cherokee 180 built in 1964. Parked side by side, the Cherokee and the curvilinear Cirrus offered a quick glimpse of the evolution of small aircraft. Aerodynamics no doubt had figured into the design of the Cherokee nearly fifty years ago, but the old girl—with her stubby fuselage, blunt nose, and "Hershey bar" wings—did seem a bit chunky next to her modern descendent. I knocked on the Cherokee's aluminum skin. Thinner than I would have imagined. It yielded to pressure almost as readily as a beer can. I eyed the propeller— maybe six feet long and a few inches broad. "Is this *really* all that moves a plane?" My inner dialogue was slipping out, carrying my anxieties with it.

"That's nothing," said Sam. "Check this out." He unlatched two extremely low-tech fasteners and lifted the hood. "It's basically a lawn mower engine with three extra cylinders."

If I replied to that comment, I don't recall what I said. More likely I was dumb-struck. But I do remember that after a beat Sam followed up his own comment. "What? How often do lawnmowers just stop for no reason?" I excused myself to make a quick phone call. I wanted to tell my wife I loved her.

Before Sam was finished with this introduction—airplane to passenger—he had one more preflight adjustment to make. He produced a role of duct tape from his flight bag, ripped off a piece, four or five inches long, and affixed it to the front "grill" of the plane. "My trusty hundred-mile-per-hour tape," he said in response to my look of astonishment. "It's cold out, so I need to restrict the airflow through the oil cooler." Then, smoothing the tape and giving this modification an approving look, he said, "Let's go save some dogs."

Having pulled the plane onto the ramp, Sam opened its only door and climbed inside. I followed, folding my six-foot-five frame into the copilot seat. Though my knees were nearly pressed against the yoke, I was careful not to touch anything, lest I accidently trip the wrong toggle. In the pilot's seat, Sam was all business and methodical self-assuredness. Even after a lifetime of takeoffs and landings, he religiously checked a preflight list kept on the dashboard. Once the prestart checklist was complete, he opened his vent window, shouted "Clear" to no one, and pressed the START button. The engine jumped to life. Then came taxi and engine run-up. When all met with his satisfaction, Sam goosed the throttle. As we accelerated down the runway and lifted off, I was reassured not just by Sam, but by the little plane's get up and go. (On a subsequent flight, Sam told me about his first plane, whose one hundred horsepower engine routinely made takeoffs "interesting.")

Sam had equipped me with a headset for cockpit communication, but I was quiet during our ascent south out of Leavenworth's army airfield on a bearing that would take us to northern Arkansas, where a homeless bloodhound awaited our arrival. Though not really familiar with cockpit protocol, I assumed shutting up on takeoff was a good idea. I watched the city of Leavenworth gradually recede, looked at the wispy morning mist hanging over the wide Missouri River, and let my eye follow the train tracks running alongside the levy. I was, inexplicably, very relaxed.

Once we reached our cruising altitude of thirty-five hundred feet, I adjusted the mouthpiece of the headset and resumed my line of questioning, working through the instruments (all analogue, most original equipment vintage 1964) on the panel one by one: "What's this do?" "How's this work?" "What's this called?" Sam resumed his role as remedial teacher and answered every query dutifully and patiently. Finally, after being informed that our airspeed was about 110 knots—or about 125 MPH—I asked another: "How slow can you fly and stay in the air?"

"I don't know," he shot back. "Do you want to find out?" No further questions—at least for a while.

I survived that mission with Sam and many others in the months that followed. Telling friends about our animal-rescue adventures in Sam's Lyndon Johnson–era plane, I'm often met with a concerned look meant, I suppose, to remind me that I have two young sons at home. I sometimes try to explain my blind confidence in Sam, but if they ever met him, no explanation would be needed. He's a pilot through and through; and after all the hours we've flown together—even through some "interesting" weather—I'm confident that even if he were flying a 1964 John Deere riding mower, he could safely land her should the engine fail at three thousand feet.

Flying with Sam has afforded me some incredible benefits, not the least of which was providing me with the perspective and experience necessary to do a credible job of writing this book. Best of all, though, has been the time spent together in flight, watching the humble, workmanlike way he goes about the business of saving dogs by moving them from point A to point B in old *November-Seven-Six-Zero-Niner-Whiskey*—and listening through the headset while a patient teacher, a top-notch pilot, and a very good man shares a small percentage of what he knows about flying and life.

Thanks, Sam.
—PR

APPENDIX

Airplanes Used in Animal Transports

Story	*Airplane*
1. "Cassidy Rides Again"	Cessna P210
2. "Home at Last, Home for Good"	Mooney M20E
	Piper PA-28 Cherokee
3. "Appetite for Aviation"	1972 Cessna 180 Skywagon
4. "Angel Gets Her Wings"	Baron B55 (Jim Carney)
	Cessna 182 (Keith Decker)
	Piper Cherokee 140 (Jim Bordoni)
	Cessna 172 (Mitchell Stafford)
5. "Mojo and Mom"	1977 Piper PA-32
6. "A Sweet Southern Girl"	Piper Aztec
7. "Pups on Approach"	Cirrus SR22
8. "A Pilot's Pilot"	Unknown
9. "Boxer, Undefeated"	1966 Piper Cherokee
	2006 Van's RV-9A
10. "Runt Triumphant"	Cessna 182
11. "Up in the Air with Uncle Jim"	Baron B55
	Cessna 182
12. "Pilot Sam Gets a Few Pointers"	1964 Piper Cherokee 180
13. "Hell on Wheels"	Piper Cherokee 140
14. "Preston"	Cessna 172
	1972 Beechcraft Baron
15. "Phoenix Rising"	Baron B55
16. "A Moving Story"	Cessna 152
17. "All-Species Airways"	Cirrus SR22
18. "Honorable Discharge"	Hawker 800
19. "Ernie's Journey"	Cessna 172
20. "Chance Encounter"	Grumman Tiger
22. "Dorie's Story"	1964 Piper Cherokee 180

23. "The Round-Tripper" — Cessna 182T
24. "Out of New Orleans" — Various
25. "Saving Christmas" — Piper Seneca II
26. "Learning to Fly" — Piper Cherokee Six / Beechcraft Bonanza

HOW YOU CAN HELP

Every year, approximately four million shelter animals are euthanized in the United States. Here are some ways you can help homeless animals find loving homes and put an end to pet overpopulation:

- Go to PilotsNPaws.org to learn more about how to volunteer as a pilot or foster-care provider.
- Contact your local animal shelter and ask how you can get involved.
- Microchip and register your pet.
- Most importantly, please be a responsible pet owner and spay/neuter your pet.

If you have your own story about an animal rescue accomplished with the help of Pilots N Paws, we'd love to consider including it in a future story collection. Please e-mail your story and contact information to dogiscopilot@gmail.com.

PHOTO CREDITS

Page vii: Jill Clover

Page xiv: Sam Taylor

Page 5: Jim Carney

Page 7: Lynn Murphy

Page 8: Louise Vickerman

Page 11: Brett Grooms; Jim Carney

Page 12: Lynn Murphy

Page 14: (top) Miles Cary

Page 15: Mike Yoder

Page 16: Marjean Greenway;
   Rhonda Mills

Page 17: Rhonda Mills; Jim Carney

Page 18: Patrick Lofvenholm

Page 20: (clockwise from top)
   Sam Taylor; Linda Schroeder;
   Jim Carney; Jim Bordoni

Page 21: Joe Radford

Page 22: Terry Fiala

Page 24–25: Mary Vitt

Page 26: (top) Mary Vitt; (bottom)
   Colleen Wyatt

Page 29: (top) Pauline Stevens

Page 30: (bottom) Tom Nalle

Page 31: (top) Caitlin Nalle; (bottom)
   Janet Plumb

Page 33: (bottom) Rhonda Miles

Page 35: (top) Jim Bordoni; (bottom)
   Keith Decker

Page 36: Jim Bordoni

Page 39–40: Devon Barger

Page 42: Sawyer Thompson

Page 44: Steve Clegg

Page 47: (bottom) Brad Elliott

Page 48: Rachel Haymes

Page 51: Robin Lee

Page 52: Stephanie Ogata

Page 55: (bottom right) Pete Howell

Page 56: Pete Howell

Page 57: Stephanie Murphy

Page 62–64: Jim Carney

Page 65: (bottom) Patrick Regan

Page 66–67: Sam Taylor

Page 69: Liza Bondarek

Page 71: Sarah Owens

Page 74: Jim Bordoni

Page 75: Sara Henderson

Page 80–81: Jim Carney

Page 82: Jim Carney; Teka Clark;
   Roxie Amsden

Page 94: Tom Scott

Page 95: (top) Glen Phelps

Page 97: (bottom) Kathy Chase

Page 99: Wanda Taylor

Page 105: Tammy Rieser

Page 110: Patrick Regan

Page 116: (top) Vicki McPherson;
   (bottom) Donna Lohmann

Page 117: Donna Lohmann

Page 118–119: Linda Gail Stevens

Page 120: Betsy Quandt

Page 121–122: Linda Gail Stevens

Page 123: (top) Linda Gail Stevens;
   (bottom) Laura Bradshaw

Page 124: Linda Gail Stevens

Page 125: Betsy Quandt

Page 132: Patrick Regan